SYNERGETIC STEW

EXPLORATIONS IN DYMAXION DINING

Cover design by Ted Ehmann
Title page drawing by Bil Baird

Thanks to the Chautauqua Institution for per-
mission to reprint recipes by Bucky's friends
printed in the Chautauqua Celebrity Cookbook.
Thanks also to National Lampoon for permis-
sion to reprint an excerpt from their January,
1972, issue.

BUCKMINSTER FULLER INSTITUTE
3501 MARKET STREET, PHILADELPHIA, PA. 19104

CONTENTS

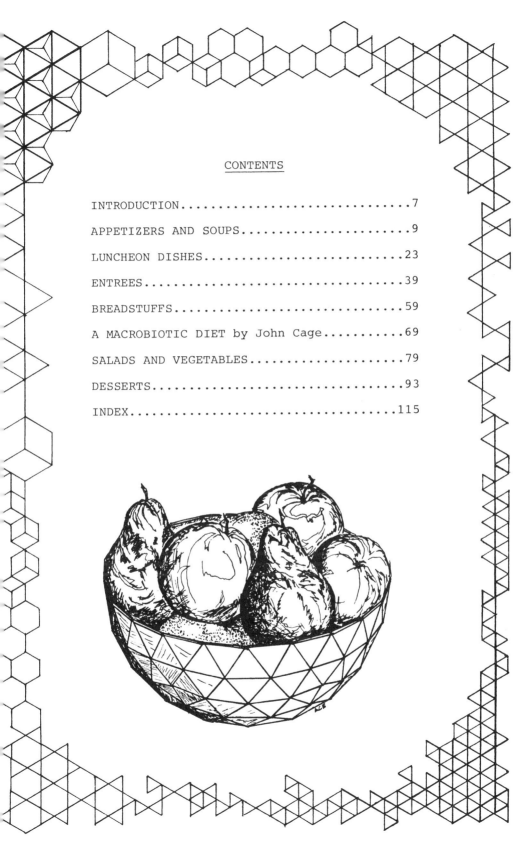

INTRODUCTION

The whole world knows Buckminster Fuller
as a design scientist, architect, author,
poet, engineer, and superb educator. Working for him is an extraordinary challenge,
calling on the "unique resource of experience
and comprehension" of each of us fortunate
enough to be in such a position. He travels
almost constantly, and comes to his home office in Philadelphia, now also the headquarters of the newly formed Buckminster Fuller
Institute, only for a few precious days a
month. And what days they are! The office,
always busy, becomes a hurricane of activity,
with several manuscripts being written and re-
written (and re-re-written). Many of the important decisions and a good part of the design projects, and that part of the month's
mail that requires Bucky's unique input, are
dealt with during these frenzied monthly
"charrettes." The copy machine runs cease-
lessly, endless cups of tea are consumed by
Bucky, endless pots of coffee consumed by the
rest of us. Sandwiches sit on our desks and
we occasionally find the time to take a bite
or two. Sometimes the work seems infinite,
yet it's somehow always finished by the time
Bucky leaves for California or Penang or London or Cincinnati, wherever his preposterous-
ly busy schedule takes him.

But the rewards are far greater than the
demands made on us. Firstly, of course, we
know that what we are doing is crucial to the
future of all humanity, that if our Spaceship
Earth has a chance of making it through this
critical time in history, it will be because
of Bucky and the message that he's been de-
livering for over fifty years. As Hugh Kenner said in Saturday Review of CRITICAL PATH:
"Making the world work, that's one short way of

5

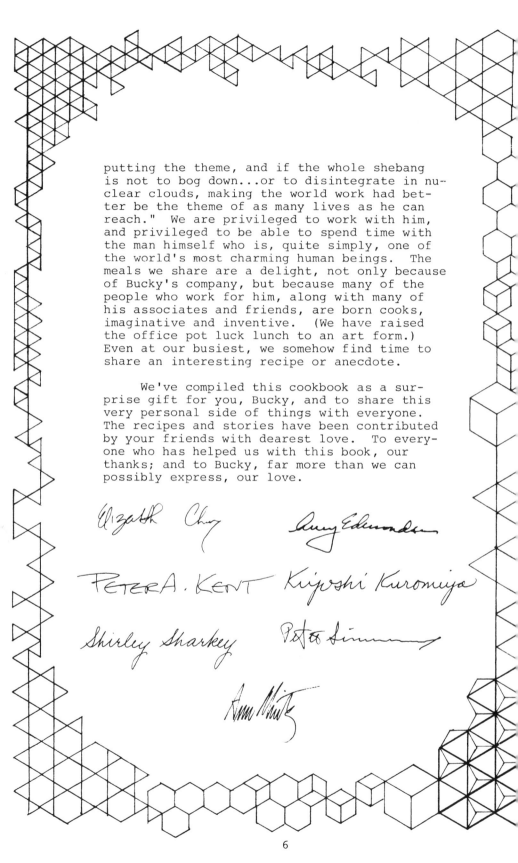

putting the theme, and if the whole shebang is not to bog down...or to disintegrate in nuclear clouds, making the world work had better be the theme of as many lives as he can reach." We are privileged to work with him, and privileged to be able to spend time with the man himself who is, quite simply, one of the world's most charming human beings. The meals we share are a delight, not only because of Bucky's company, but because many of the people who work for him, along with many of his associates and friends, are born cooks, imaginative and inventive. (We have raised the office pot luck lunch to an art form.) Even at our busiest, we somehow find time to share an interesting recipe or anecdote.

We've compiled this cookbook as a surprise gift for you, Bucky, and to share this very personal side of things with everyone. The recipes and stories have been contributed by your friends with dearest love. To everyone who has helped us with this book, our thanks; and to Bucky, far more than we can possibly express, our love.

Elizabeth Chey

Amy Edmondson

Peter A. Kent

Kiyoshi Kuromiya

Shirley Sharkey

Peter Simms

Ann White

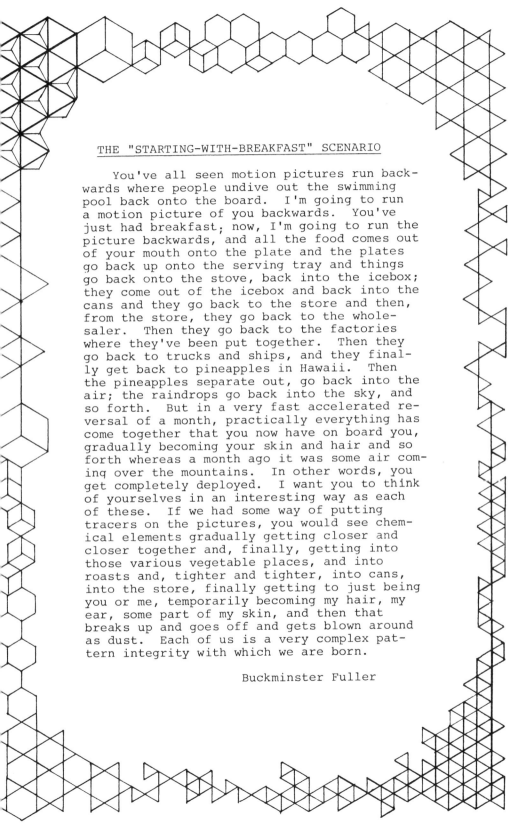

THE "STARTING-WITH-BREAKFAST" SCENARIO

You've all seen motion pictures run backwards where people undive out the swimming pool back onto the board. I'm going to run a motion picture of you backwards. You've just had breakfast; now, I'm going to run the picture backwards, and all the food comes out of your mouth onto the plate and the plates go back up onto the serving tray and things go back onto the stove, back into the icebox; they come out of the icebox and back into the cans and they go back to the store and then, from the store, they go back to the wholesaler. Then they go back to the factories where they've been put together. Then they go back to trucks and ships, and they finally get back to pineapples in Hawaii. Then the pineapples separate out, go back into the air; the raindrops go back into the sky, and so forth. But in a very fast accelerated reversal of a month, practically everything has come together that you now have on board you, gradually becoming your skin and hair and so forth whereas a month ago it was some air coming over the mountains. In other words, you get completely deployed. I want you to think of yourselves in an interesting way as each of these. If we had some way of putting tracers on the pictures, you would see chemical elements gradually getting closer and closer together and, finally, getting into those various vegetable places, and into roasts and, tighter and tighter, into cans, into the store, finally getting to just being you or me, temporarily becoming my hair, my ear, some part of my skin, and then that breaks up and goes off and gets blown around as dust. Each of us is a very complex pattern integrity with which we are born.

Buckminster Fuller

BUCKY PIE

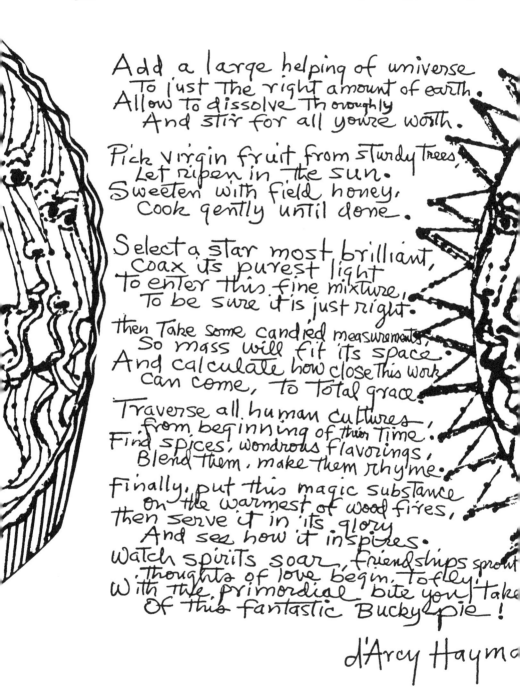

Add a large helping of universe
   To just the right amount of earth.
Allow to dissolve Thoroughly
   And stir for all you're worth.

Pick virgin fruit from sturdy trees,
   Let ripen in the sun.
Sweeten with field honey,
   Cook gently until done.

Select a star most brilliant,
   Coax its purest light
To enter this fine mixture,
   To be sure it is just right.

Then Take some candied measurements,
   So mass will fit its space.
And calculate how close This work
   Can come, To Total grace.

Traverse all human cultures,
   from beginning of their Time.
Find spices, wondrous flavorings,
   Blend them, make them rhyme.

Finally, put this magic substance
   on the warmest of wood fires,
Then serve it in its glory
   And see how it inspires.
Watch spirits soar, friendships sprout
   Thoughts of love begin, Tofley!
With the primordial bite you! take
   Of this fantastic Bucky pie!

                    d'Arcy Hayma

8

APPETIZERS AND SOUPS

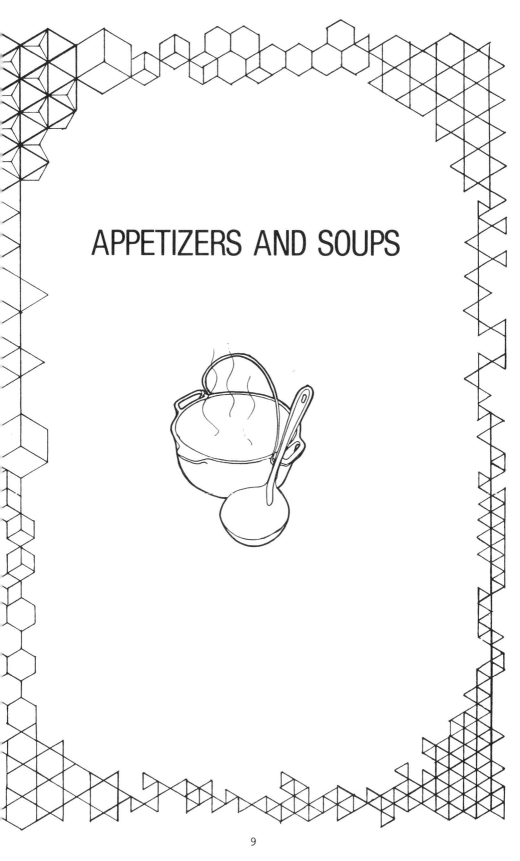

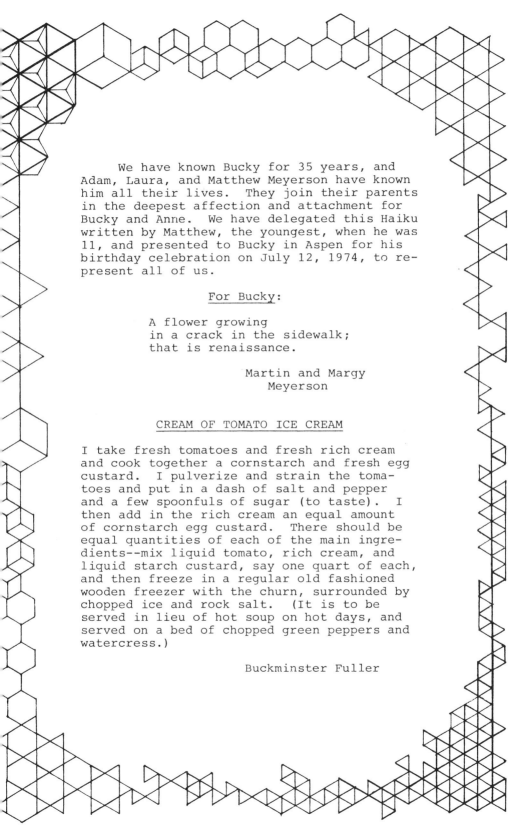

We have known Bucky for 35 years, and
Adam, Laura, and Matthew Meyerson have known
him all their lives. They join their parents
in the deepest affection and attachment for
Bucky and Anne. We have delegated this Haiku
written by Matthew, the youngest, when he was
11, and presented to Bucky in Aspen for his
birthday celebration on July 12, 1974, to re-
present all of us.

For Bucky:

A flower growing
in a crack in the sidewalk;
that is renaissance.

Martin and Margy
Meyerson

CREAM OF TOMATO ICE CREAM

I take fresh tomatoes and fresh rich cream
and cook together a cornstarch and fresh egg
custard. I pulverize and strain the tomatoes and put in a dash of salt and pepper
and a few spoonfuls of sugar (to taste). I
then add in the rich cream an equal amount
of cornstarch egg custard. There should be
equal quantities of each of the main ingre-
dients--mix liquid tomato, rich cream, and
liquid starch custard, say one quart of each,
and then freeze in a regular old fashioned
wooden freezer with the churn, surrounded by
chopped ice and rock salt. (It is to be
served in lieu of hot soup on hot days, and
served on a bed of chopped green peppers and
watercress.)

Buckminster Fuller

Buckminster Fuller's

Repair Manual for the Entire Universe

reconstituted by Henry Beard, Harry Fischman, and Jeffrey Prescott

Excerpt from National Lampoon, January, 1972.

Repaired clam (Dymaxion Bivalve Module). Even the discontinuous observer can instantly apprehend the significant, repair-worthy, design deficiencies in the classic mollusk living-unit: From the clam-view, the structure looms as an asymmetrical, weighty, hollow stone, composed of timed deposit-accretions of a number of substances, the result being a bony agglomeration that prevents effective tide-borne global gloaming-roaming without, paradoxically, providing sufficient internal strength to resist penetration efforts by predators, a fact demonstrated to my satisfaction at the age of two, by seagulls, whom I used to watch in Maine (during an hiatus in my since-abandoned researches into a motor that would run on ordinary tree moss) bombing shore rocks with members of the local quahog population, in invariably successful attempts at break-and-entry. From the man-view, besides the directly resulting loss of a husbanded resource, the asymmetrical, unarticulated shell-shape complicates preconsumption storage in eatingry places; makes access without appropriate tools to the chew-worthy, hors d'oeuvral body all but impossible; negates efficient hexamerous (order-of-six) or dodecamerous (order-of-twelve) arrangement of the eventually halved appetizery item on circular platters; and leaves as the end-product two randomly concave hemispheres which make notoriously inefficient ashtrays, their only conceivable post-clam-habitational use. Yet, apart from specialized local structural variations occasioned by evolutionary pressures and other minor differentiations from the basic matrix, the underlying pattern has existed unchanged for upwards of fifty million years. Obviously, this is something of a record for clinging to an outmoded housing system.

The repair I have indicated here eliminates the enumerated deficiencies and simultaneously provides numerous bonuses. First, the dymaxion tensional-sectional construction, which, appropriately enough, uses as its main structural material ground-up clamshells, will resist traumatic impact overpressures of a size unlikely to be inflicted by any seagull not capable of a sustained Mach 2.3 dive from fifteen thousand feet and entails one-fifth the cost of duplication of the original shell; second, handles have been emplaced on both dymaxial hemispheres for simplified post-harvesting clam-extraction, a convenience which in no way renders the clam vulnerable to sea-occurring predators (this does not include my proposed Dymaxion 4-D Dolphin, the introduction of which in large numbers would necessitate minor redesign—see *Geodada*, p. 157), since the hinged hemispheres adhere with a high-integrity spring-and-suction closure; and, third, flat top-and-bottom surfaces permit efficient space-utilization, both in the seafood store and on the seabed floor, vastly increase snack-on-platter placement efficiencies, and transform the heretofore marginally usable half-shells into attractive receptacles for gears, vectors, trusses, vertices, and other randoming doodads. In addition, the regular rim-crenellation, introduced originally as a perimetric strengthening factor, provides handy out-of-mouth cigarette cradles when the dymaxion shells are used in an asthraical mode.

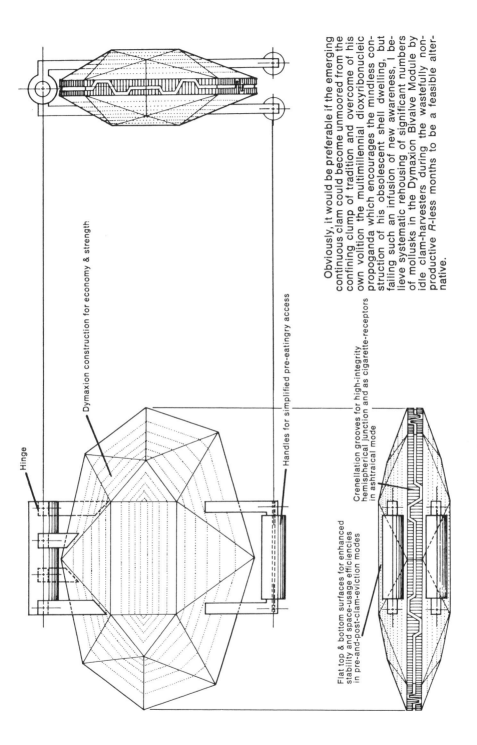

Hinge

Dymaxion construction for economy & strength

Handles for simplified pre-eatingry access

Crenellation grooves for high-integrity hemispherical junction and as cigarette-receptors in ashtraical mode

Flat top & bottom surfaces for enhanced stability and space-usage efficiencies in pre-and-post-clam-eviction modes

Obviously, it would be preferable if the emerging continuous clam could become unmoored from the confining clump of tradition and overcome of his own volition the multimillennial dioxyribonucleic propoganda which encourages the mindless construction of his obsolescent shell dwelling, but failing such an infusion of new awareness, I believe systematic rehousing of significant numbers of mollusks in the Dymaxion Bivalve Module by idle clam-harvesters during the wastefully non-productive R-less months to be a feasible alternative.

As you travel in Spaceship Earth,
Alone or in a group,
Remember, the cure for all your ills
Is just plain old

CHICKEN SOUP

4 lbs. stewing chicken (cut up, include giz-
   ard, heart, neck, and feet)
2 qts. cold water
1 large onion (cut in half)
2 carrots (cut in half)
1 root parsley (soup green with root) (cut in
   half)
1 small parsnip (cut in half)
2 pieces of dill
salt and pepper to taste

Remove excess fat from pieces of chicken.
Place chicken in water, bring to boil. Add
onion, parsnip, carrots, and root of parsley.
Simmer covered, until chicken is tender
(about 1½ hours). Tie soup greens and dill
together with white thread and put into soup.
Simmer for 15 minutes. Remove greens. Add
seasoning to taste. Soup may be strained.
Chicken may be cut up and added to soup.

Guaranteed to give you SYNERGY.

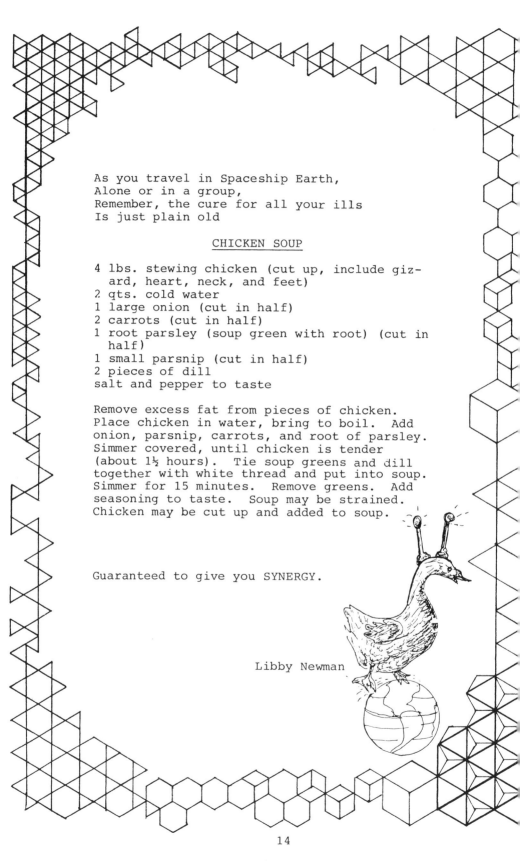

Libby Newman

14

POSITIVELY PUMPKIN BISQUE

1 16 oz. can pumpkin
½ cup sour cream
2 cups canned chicken broth
1 cup light cream
¼ tsp. mace
1 medium size onion, finely chopped
1 Tbs. real lemon rind

Cold Cooking Instructions: In pan saute
onion in butter until soft. In large mixing
bowl add pumpkin, sauteed onion, sour cream,
chicken broth, mace, lemon rind, and light
cream. Put into blender and puree. Cover
and chill. Before serving, garnish with dol-
lops of additional sour cream and sprinkle
with chopped watercress.

Hot Cooking Instructions: In large saucepan
saute onion in butter. When soft, add pumpkin,
chicken broth, sour cream, mace, and lemon
rind. Stirring constantly, bring to a boil.
Add light cream right before serving, bring
to a boil. Before serving, garnish as above.
Serves 6 to 8. This recipe contains no salt.
Salt to taste at your own risk.

Ted Ehmann

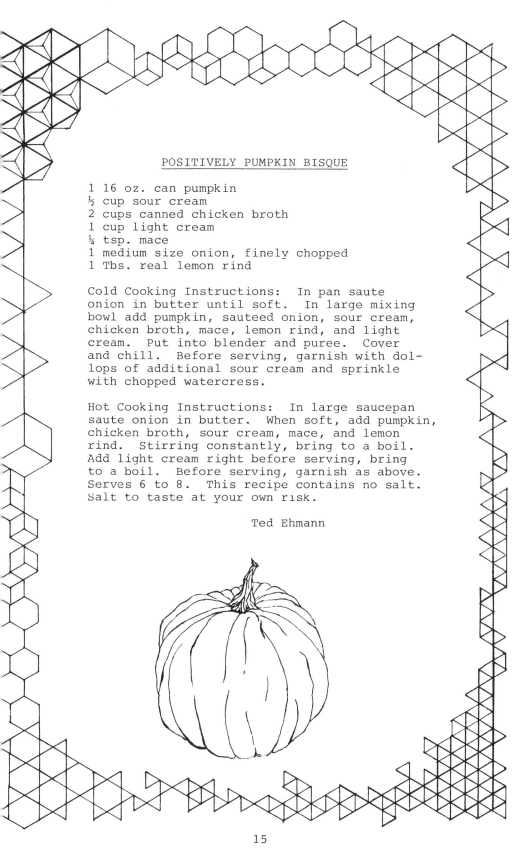

CHEESE TETRAHEDRON

623.10 **Cheese Tetrahedron**: If we take a symmetrical polyhedron of cheese, such as a cube, and slice parallel to one of its faces, what is left over is no longer symmetrical; it is no longer a cube. Slice one face of a cheese octahedron, and what is left over is no longer symmetrical; it is no longer an octahedron. If you try slicing parallel to one of the faces of all the symmetrical geometries, i.e., all the Platonic and Archimedean "solids," each made of cheese, what is left after the parallel slice is removed is no longer the same symmetrical polyhedron—but with one exception, the tetrahedron.

> Buckminster Fuller,
> from SYNERGETICS

1. Take a piece of hard cheese.
2. Cut in the shape of a tetrahedron as follows:
   - Six equivalent edges (any length you choose--conceptuality is independent of size)
   - Four vertices
   - Four faces
   - Face angles 60°
   - Center angles 109.16°
3. Slice parallel to any one of the four faces of the cheese tetrahedron.
4. Eat the flat piece.
5. Notice that the remaining cheese is still a tetrahedron, omni-symmetrical and undistorted by your slicing.
6. Reflect on the fact that the tetrahedron is the only structure for which this is true.

Amy Edmondson

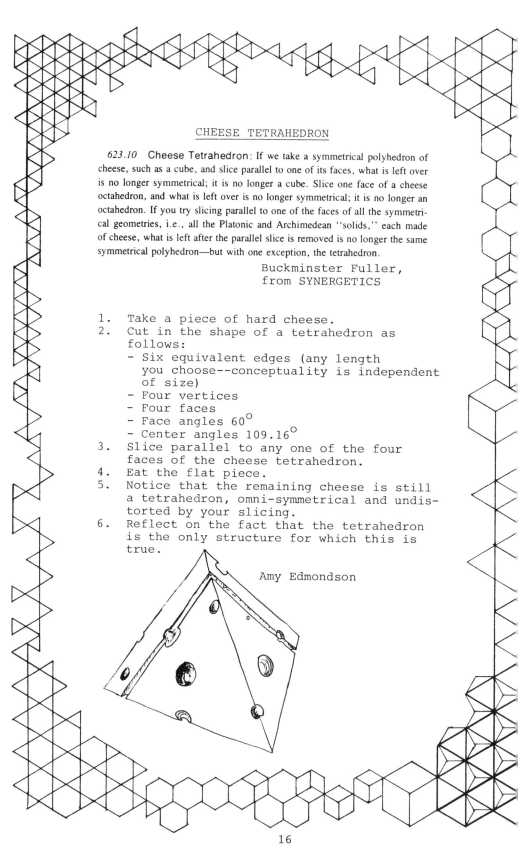

FRANKLIN HOUSE SHRIMP SCAMPI

1 lb. shrimp--25 to 30 shrimp/lb. size
2 lbs. drained Italian roasted peppers
   (Note: these are an essential ingredient)
¼ cup olive oil
6 large cloves of garlic, minced
4 large shallots
1 Tbs. fresh lemon juice
¼ cup dry white wine
½ tsp. freshly ground black pepper
¼ tsp. Worcestershire sauce
¼ lb. sweet butter, cut into ½" cubes
1 Tbs. chopped parsley

First prepare all of the ingredients. If this is done several hours in advance, everything must be kept cold and airtight. Peel, devein, and split the shrimp (butterfly them) so that they are flat and in one piece. Cut drained peppers into 1" x 1½" rectangular pieces and saute in hot olive oil until some are dark brown and a few are black. Drain and set aside.

Put butter, shrimp, garlic, and shallots into a saute pan and saute all together. When the shrimp start to turn pink, add lemon juice, white wine, peppers, and Worcestershire sauce. When the shrimp turn to a clear white color, add the parsley and salt and pepper to taste. This whole process should take about 10 to 15 minutes and <u>care must be taken not to overcook</u> shrimp.

For an appetizer, serve on a plate with French bread or bread sticks. If serving as an entree, serve on a bed of white and green fetuccine noodles or with rice. Either way, serve 2 or 3 favorite vegetables and French bread or bread sticks.

by Dennis Tyler,
contributed by
Werner Erhard

ED MUSKIE'S FISH CHOWDER

¼ lb. salt pork, diced
2 onions, sliced or diced
4 cups of potatoes, in small pieces
1 or 2 cups of water
2 lbs. haddock
1 tsp. salt
¼ tsp. pepper
¼ tsp. Ac'cent
2 cups whole milk
1 tall can of evaporated milk

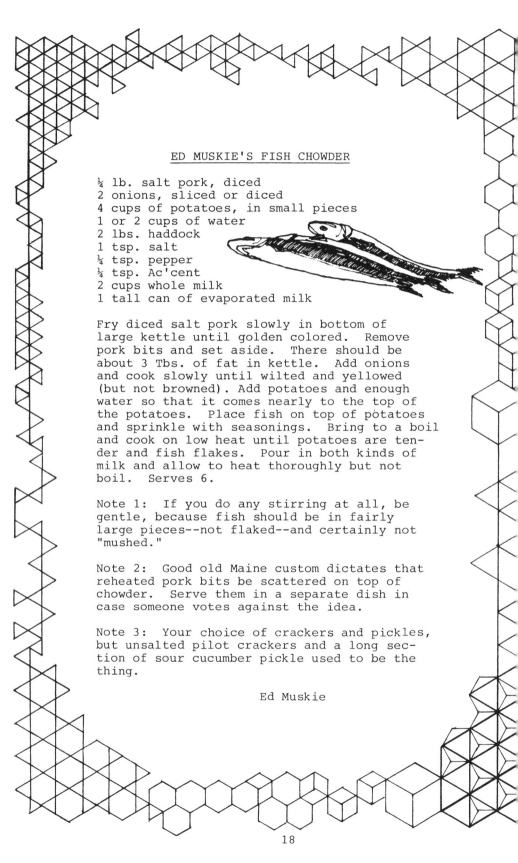

Fry diced salt pork slowly in bottom of
large kettle until golden colored. Remove
pork bits and set aside. There should be
about 3 Tbs. of fat in kettle. Add onions
and cook slowly until wilted and yellowed
(but not browned). Add potatoes and enough
water so that it comes nearly to the top of
the potatoes. Place fish on top of potatoes
and sprinkle with seasonings. Bring to a boil
and cook on low heat until potatoes are tender and fish flakes. Pour in both kinds of
milk and allow to heat thoroughly but not
boil. Serves 6.

Note 1: If you do any stirring at all, be
gentle, because fish should be in fairly
large pieces--not flaked--and certainly not
"mushed."

Note 2: Good old Maine custom dictates that
reheated pork bits be scattered on top of
chowder. Serve them in a separate dish in
case someone votes against the idea.

Note 3: Your choice of crackers and pickles,
but unsalted pilot crackers and a long sec-
tion of sour cucumber pickle used to be the
thing.

Ed Muskie

I'll never forget my first half hour as Bucky's secretary. We said hello, he said he wanted to dictate something, and I took out my pen. Then he started at breakneck speed with: "The omni-directional inter-accomodative comprehensively rememberable Scheherazade number is...". By that point, I was watching my right hand furiously scribble across the page, while waving with my left hand to get him to slow down. (Of course anyone who knows Bucky better than I did at the time knows he closes his eyes when he's concentrating.) Anyway, five minutes later I looked up, realized Bucky had no idea how lost I was, and boldly asked him to start over-- "Oh, of course, darling."

Now that I'm more relaxed I occasionally even find time to whip up:

OMNI-DIRECTIONAL, INTER-ACCOMODATIVE/COMPRE-HENSIVELY REMEMBERABLE CHEESE TETRASCROLLS

¼ lb. (6) Filo leaves
6 Tbs. melted butter
6 oz. any spiced semi-soft cheese (Boursin, Alouette, Rondele, etc.)

Thaw filo leaves according to package directions. Preheat oven to 400°. Carefully lay one 12" x 16" filo sheet on countertop, brush with melted butter, top with second sheet, cut into 8 12" x 2" strips. Put ½ tablespoon cheese on corner of strip and roll in tetrascroll fashion to form triangular appetizers. Place on buttered cookie sheet, brush tops with melted butter and bake for 10 minutes. Serve hot. Makes 24.

Shirley Sharkey

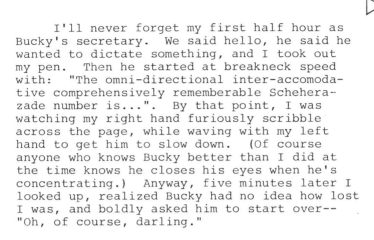

etc...   until ↗

19

ROMANY MARIE'S, 1929

I first met Mr. Fuller, as I used to
call him, at Romany Marie's in 1929. Bucky
was in a continual state of dialectic creat-
ivity, giving talks in any situation before
any kind of audience. He would talk to me
as to a throng, walking and talking every-
where--over the Brooklyn Bridge, over innum-
erable cups of coffee. Bucky drank everything--
tea, coffee, liquor--with equal gusto and would
often be in a state of wide-eyed euphoria for
three days straight. He had become a God-
possessed man, like a Messiah of ideas. He
was a prophet of things to come. Bucky didn't
take care of himself, but always had amazing
strength. He often went without sleep for
several days, and he didn't always eat either.

Isamu Noguchi

I made some furniture to decorate Romany
Marie's in the Village, and she would give me
a meal every day instead of money. She would
keep a big pot of vegetable soup cooking all
the time, constantly adding water and pieces
of meat. It was delicious but I didn't want
to overdo it, so I only came every other night.
There I would stay, a table sitter, all
evening, until very late into the night. It
was the Greenwich Village of the late 1920's
and early 1930's that generated great new
thinking. I gained many friends for my con-
cepts and lost none.

Buckminster Fuller

MARIE'S ROUMANIAN TCHOURBA

Romany Marie's mainstay meal served to the many struggling artists and scientists who frequented her memorable Greenwich Village cafe.

Serves 6 to 8.

1 lb. chopped round steak	2½ qts. water
1 cup chopped celery	3 large carrots
2 cups diced raw potatoes	1 leek
1 cup cut string beans	½ cup diced onion
1 cup stewed tomatoes	1 Tbs. parsley
2 cloves pressed garlic	salt, pepper
	fresh dill

Prepare 1" meat balls of round steak. (If purse is small, buy hamburger.) Dredge with flour and put aside.

Fill large soup pot with water and bring to a boil. Add all other ingredients. Cover and cook for 1½ hours. Add meat balls to soup and simmer for one more hour.

When serving, sprinkle fresh dill liberally (very important for Tchourba) over soup. This is a very satisfying and nutritious meal designed to fill the empty stomach and fit for a king when served with mountains of black bread and sweet butter.

Paula Martin

Paula Martin was an artists' model in New York in the 1920's and 30's, and was a waitress at Romany Marie's.

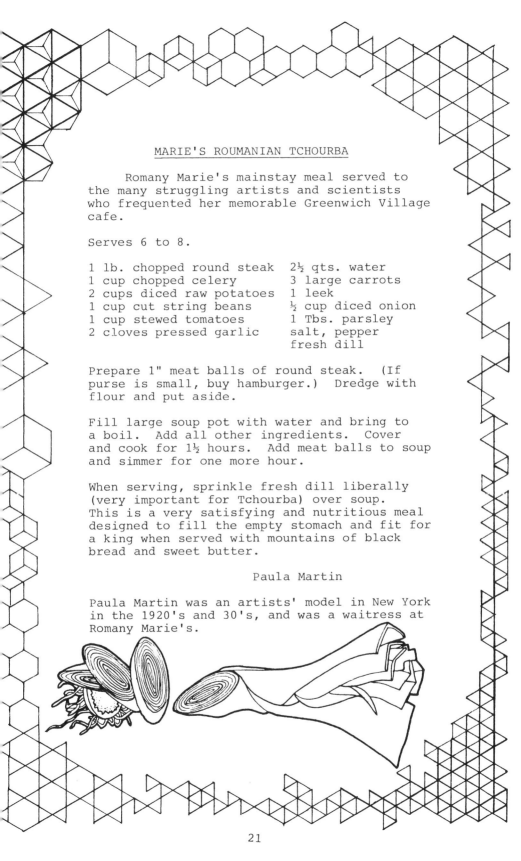

21

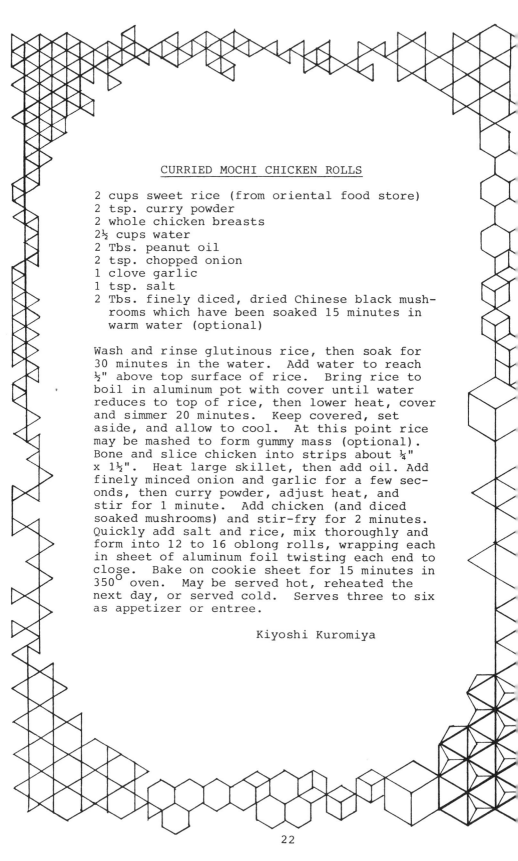

CURRIED MOCHI CHICKEN ROLLS

2 cups sweet rice (from oriental food store)
2 tsp. curry powder
2 whole chicken breasts
2½ cups water
2 Tbs. peanut oil
2 tsp. chopped onion
1 clove garlic
1 tsp. salt
2 Tbs. finely diced, dried Chinese black mushrooms which have been soaked 15 minutes in
  warm water (optional)

Wash and rinse glutinous rice, then soak for
30 minutes in the water. Add water to reach
½" above top surface of rice. Bring rice to
boil in aluminum pot with cover until water
reduces to top of rice, then lower heat, cover
and simmer 20 minutes. Keep covered, set
aside, and allow to cool. At this point rice
may be mashed to form gummy mass (optional).
Bone and slice chicken into strips about ¼"
x 1½". Heat large skillet, then add oil. Add
finely minced onion and garlic for a few sec-
onds, then curry powder, adjust heat, and
stir for 1 minute. Add chicken (and diced
soaked mushrooms) and stir-fry for 2 minutes.
Quickly add salt and rice, mix thoroughly and
form into 12 to 16 oblong rolls, wrapping each
in sheet of aluminum foil twisting each end to
close. Bake on cookie sheet for 15 minutes in
350° oven. May be served hot, reheated the
next day, or served cold. Serves three to six
as appetizer or entree.

Kiyoshi Kuromiya

22

LUNCHEON DISHES

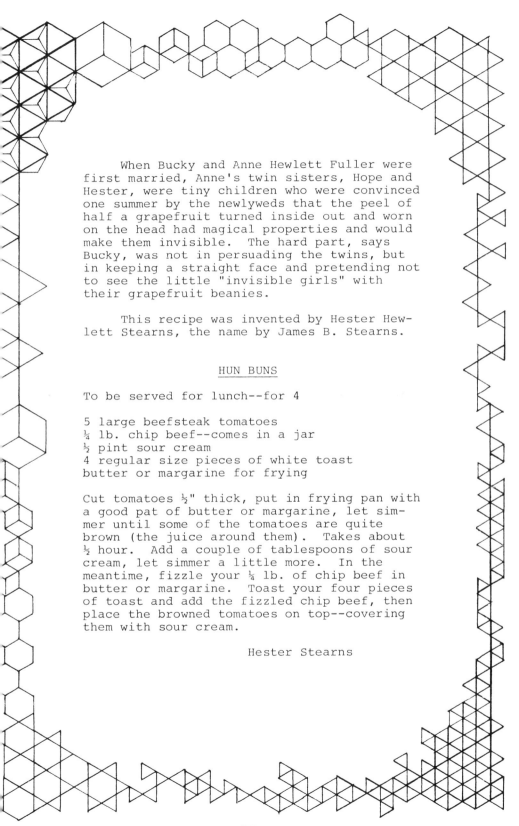

When Bucky and Anne Hewlett Fuller were first married, Anne's twin sisters, Hope and Hester, were tiny children who were convinced one summer by the newlyweds that the peel of half a grapefruit turned inside out and worn on the head had magical properties and would make them invisible. The hard part, says Bucky, was not in persuading the twins, but in keeping a straight face and pretending not to see the little "invisible girls" with their grapefruit beanies.

This recipe was invented by Hester Hewlett Stearns, the name by James B. Stearns.

HUN BUNS

To be served for lunch--for 4

5 large beefsteak tomatoes
¼ lb. chip beef--comes in a jar
½ pint sour cream
4 regular size pieces of white toast
butter or margarine for frying

Cut tomatoes ½" thick, put in frying pan with a good pat of butter or margarine, let simmer until some of the tomatoes are quite brown (the juice around them). Takes about ½ hour. Add a couple of tablespoons of sour cream, let simmer a little more. In the meantime, fizzle your ¼ lb. of chip beef in butter or margarine. Toast your four pieces of toast and add the fizzled chip beef, then place the browned tomatoes on top--covering them with sour cream.

Hester Stearns

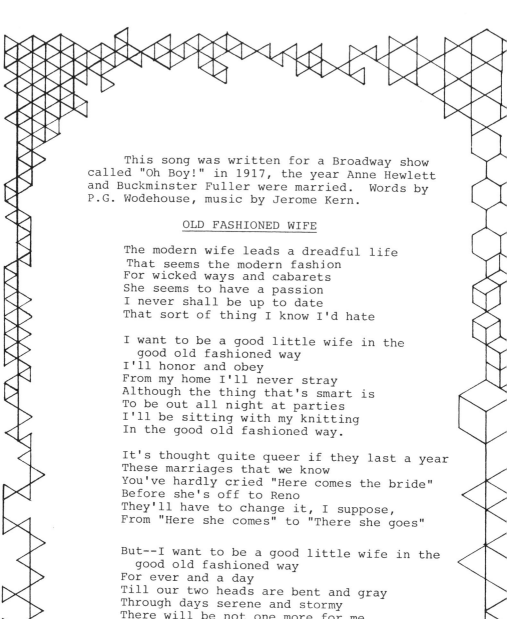

This song was written for a Broadway show called "Oh Boy!" in 1917, the year Anne Hewlett and Buckminster Fuller were married. Words by P.G. Wodehouse, music by Jerome Kern.

OLD FASHIONED WIFE

The modern wife leads a dreadful life
That seems the modern fashion
For wicked ways and cabarets
She seems to have a passion
I never shall be up to date
That sort of thing I know I'd hate

I want to be a good little wife in the
  good old fashioned way
I'll honor and obey
From my home I'll never stray
Although the thing that's smart is
To be out all night at parties
I'll be sitting with my knitting
In the good old fashioned way.

It's thought quite queer if they last a year
These marriages that we know
You've hardly cried "Here comes the bride"
Before she's off to Reno
They'll have to change it, I suppose,
From "Here she comes" to "There she goes"

But--I want to be a good little wife in the
  good old fashioned way
For ever and a day
Till our two heads are bent and gray
Through days serene and stormy
There will be not one more for me,
And we'll weather by together
In the good old fashioned way

Hope Watts

POEM FOR ALLEGRA

June 4, 1931

I'll tell you a story 'bout Goldy Lox
How she once hid in the Lox ice box.
It wasn't a modern Frigidaire,
But the old lump style that is now so rare.
If it hadn't been an old fashioned one
The end of this story would be no fun.
For she ate all the butter
And lots of the lamb
And then finished off on a tumbler of jam.
This made queer things happen in Goldy's
plump tummy,
And loudly she called,
"Please come get me, Mummy."
Then suddenly Goldy began to smother
And frightened, she shrieked for her
precious mother.
Though Mrs. Lox heard the muffled scream,
She thought the noise just some souring cream.
Just then the ice man came along,
And said, "Mrs. Lox, there's something wrong.
Inside the box, I hear queer squeaking,
And from all the cracks, the food is leaking.
But strangest of all, the dang thing's
Speaking."
Whereat Mrs. Lox threw open the door
And out rolled Goldy on the floor
Saying, "Oh, Mummy, I've such a pain,
I promise I'll never do it again."

Buckminster Fuller

27

ONION-MAYONNAISE FRENCH BREAD TOAST

1 large onion
½ cup mayonnaise
salt and pepper to taste

Chop onion into ½" pieces or finer. Combine
with mayonnaise, salt, and pepper.

Spread over sliced pieces of French bread.
Place in broiler until golden brown. Serve.
Be careful not to burn your mouth.

Variation: add cheese.

Ruth Asawa Lanier

CLAM TEMPURA

1 egg
1 tsp. oil
½ cup flour
2 8 oz. cans clams
4 Tbs. clam juice

Mix all ingredients together. (The egg can be
separated and the white whipped until stiff,
but I usually don't bother.) Let stand for
45 minutes. Fry by spoonfuls in hot oil.
Serve with rice and dipping sauce made with
tamari, sweet sherry or rice wine (Mirin),
grated fresh ginger, 1 teaspoon each white
vinegar and sugar, and red pepper.

Ann Mintz

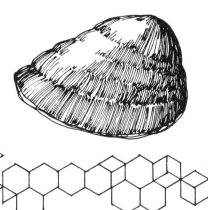

PACIFIC PALISADES SHRIMP SALAD

As served and enjoyed poolside on many a sunny Southern California day at Bucky and Anne's Pacific Palisades home.

2 ripe avocados
¼ lb. cooked baby shrimp
2-3 Tbs. mayonnaise
1/3 tsp. ground cumin
squeeze lemon juice
pinch paprika
Boston head lettuce
salt and freshly ground pepper to taste

Mash avocados with mayonnaise to consistency of porridge, then add shrimp to mixture. Add cumin, ground pepper to taste, and salt if necessary. Serve on leaf of Boston lettuce sprinkled with lemon juice, with pinch of paprika atop mound for color. May be served with wholewheat toast points or steamed, buttered, and rolled flour or cornmeal tortillas.

Kiyoshi Kuromiya

© Buckminster Fuller

WORLD RESOURCES INVENTORY PIZZA

On top of a United States frozen pizza, add:

Chunks of Greek Feta cheese
Brazilian green pepper
dash of African cayenne
dash of Indian curry
dash of Chinese ginger
dash of Russian dill
dash of French garlic
dash of Columbian chili pepper (Mexican will
  do in a pinch)
a tiny sprinkle of Pacific Ocean sea salt

Bake at 350° for 20 minutes. Serve with
Australian lemonade chilled with Antarctic
ice.

                    Medard Gabel

OMNI-TRIANGULATED OMELETTE

2 eggs, without shells
1-2 squirts of milk

Combine above ingredients in bowl, beat well.
Put in buttered frying pan. Add:

Feta cheese (the more the better)
basil (lots)

Adding the basil is the only tricky part. For
maximum effect it needs to be sprinkled on in
an omni-triangulated pattern. This can either
be quickly accomplished or very slowly. The
slow method runs the risk of burning the omelette. The slow method is to place the flakes
of basil down in lines either one at a time
(the very slow method) or else by using a
piece of notebook paper rolled into a funnel
and depositing the basil in lines with this
trusty device. The quickly accomplished
method is to rapidly sprinkle just enough basil
onto the cooking omelette and then stand back
and stare at the congealing omelette until you
see the omni-triangulated pattern.

Serve when done.

Medard Gabel

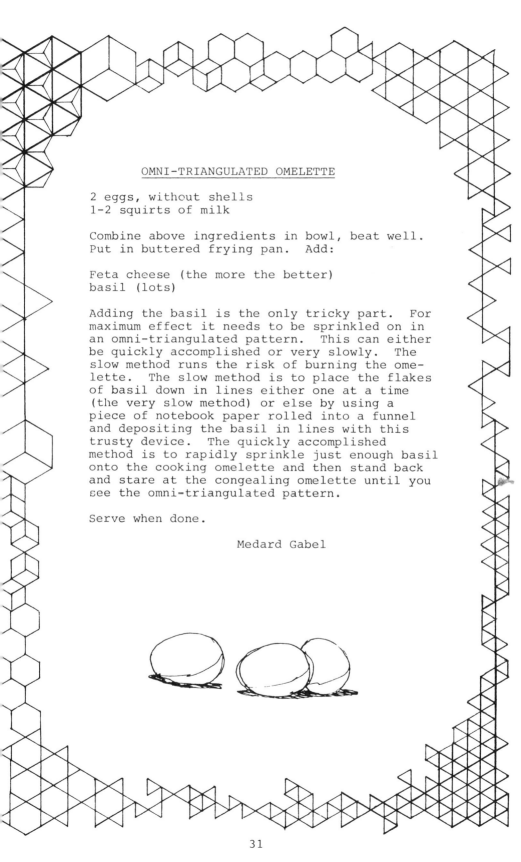

31

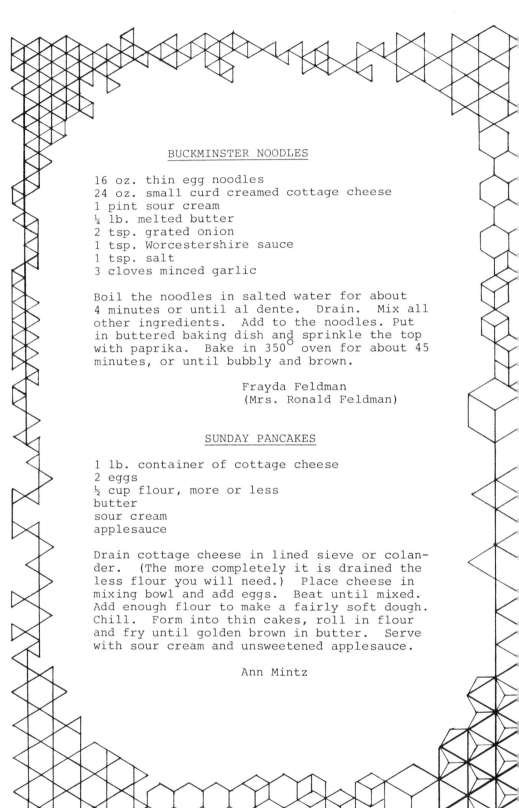

BUCKMINSTER NOODLES

16 oz. thin egg noodles
24 oz. small curd creamed cottage cheese
1 pint sour cream
¼ lb. melted butter
2 tsp. grated onion
1 tsp. Worcestershire sauce
1 tsp. salt
3 cloves minced garlic

Boil the noodles in salted water for about 4 minutes or until al dente. Drain. Mix all other ingredients. Add to the noodles. Put in buttered baking dish and sprinkle the top with paprika. Bake in 350° oven for about 45 minutes, or until bubbly and brown.

Frayda Feldman
(Mrs. Ronald Feldman)

SUNDAY PANCAKES

1 lb. container of cottage cheese
2 eggs
½ cup flour, more or less
butter
sour cream
applesauce

Drain cottage cheese in lined sieve or colander. (The more completely it is drained the less flour you will need.) Place cheese in mixing bowl and add eggs. Beat until mixed. Add enough flour to make a fairly soft dough. Chill. Form into thin cakes, roll in flour and fry until golden brown in butter. Serve with sour cream and unsweetened applesauce.

Ann Mintz

To work off those dymaxion calories, here is the recipe for a Scottish Country Dance, the _Tensegrity Reel_, written in honor of Buckminster's eighty-fifth birthday by Arthur Loeb:

Bars:

1-2 First man and third lady change places by the right hand.

3-4 First and third ladies, as well as first and third man, cross by the left hand.

5-6 First lady and third man change places by the right hand.

7-8 First and third couples cross by the left hand.

9-10 Second couple Petronella turn; first and third couples change places with each other by the right hand.

11-12 All three couples set in two rows across the dance.

13-14 Second couple Petronella turn, while others cross by the right hand.

15-16 All set, taking hands along the sides of the dance.

17-18 Second couple Petronella turn; first and third couples change places with each other by the right hand.

19-20 All three couples set in two rows across the dance.

21-22 Second couple Petronella turn, while others cross by the right hand.

23-24 All set, taking hands along the sides of the dance.

25-26 First lady and third man change places by the right hand.

27-28 First and third ladies, as well as first and third man, cross by the left hand.

29-30 First man and third lady change places by the right hand.

31-32 First and third couples cross by the left hand.

33—40 First and second couples poussette.

First danced by the Harvard Scottish Country Dancers in the Spring of 1980. Newly notated October 18, 1982. Arthur Loeb

WHAT ONE MAN CAN DO

I suppose that there are those
Who will say he had it easy,
Had it made in fact
Before he'd even begun.
They don't know
the things I know,
For I was always with him.
It may sound strange
But we were more than friends.
It's hard to try and tell the truth,
When no one wants to listen,
When no one seems to care
what's going on.
It's hard to stand alone
When you need someone beside you,
Your spirit and your faith,
They must be strong.
What one man can do is dream,
What one man can do is love.
What one man can do is change the
    world,
And make it new again.
Don't you see
What one man can do?
That's how bright his mind is,
That's how strong his love for
you and me.
A friend to all the universe,
Grandfather of the future,
And everything that
I would like to be.
What one man can do is dream,
What one man can do is love.
What one man can do is change the
    world,
And make it young again.
Can't you see what one man can do?

Written for Bucky's 85th
birthday by John Denver

34

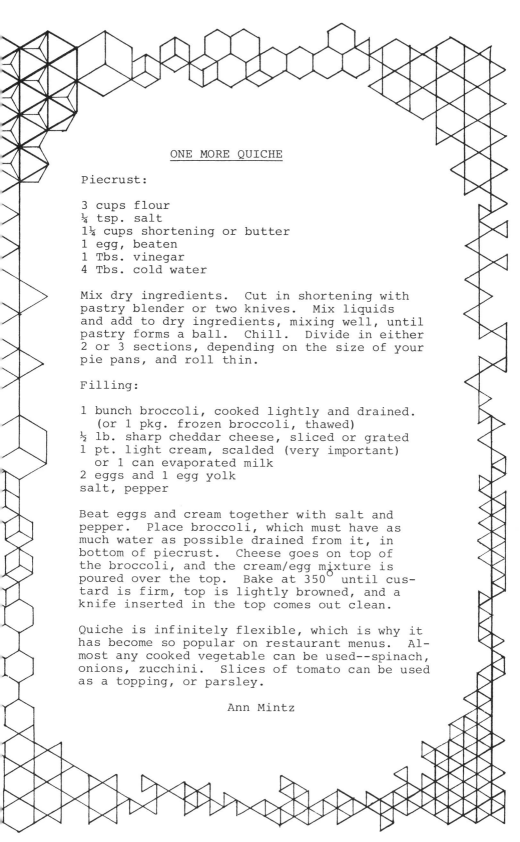

ONE MORE QUICHE

Piecrust:

3 cups flour
¼ tsp. salt
1¼ cups shortening or butter
1 egg, beaten
1 Tbs. vinegar
4 Tbs. cold water

Mix dry ingredients. Cut in shortening with
pastry blender or two knives. Mix liquids
and add to dry ingredients, mixing well, until
pastry forms a ball. Chill. Divide in either
2 or 3 sections, depending on the size of your
pie pans, and roll thin.

Filling:

1 bunch broccoli, cooked lightly and drained.
   (or 1 pkg. frozen broccoli, thawed)
½ lb. sharp cheddar cheese, sliced or grated
1 pt. light cream, scalded (very important)
   or 1 can evaporated milk
2 eggs and 1 egg yolk
salt, pepper

Beat eggs and cream together with salt and
pepper. Place broccoli, which must have as
much water as possible drained from it, in
bottom of piecrust. Cheese goes on top of
the broccoli, and the cream/egg mixture is
poured over the top. Bake at 350° until custard is firm, top is lightly browned, and a
knife inserted in the top comes out clean.

Quiche is infinitely flexible, which is why it
has become so popular on restaurant menus. Almost any cooked vegetable can be used--spinach,
onions, zucchini. Slices of tomato can be used
as a topping, or parsley.

Ann Mintz

NO MORE SECONDHAND CATSUP

Early in the 1920's, when enclosed area product uniting was as yet envisioned locally in conceptualizations formalized by bottle-canry availabilities, package-uniting of catsup and its tomato condiment alikenesses was understood to be a function of the glass bottle.

This silicone vesselizing as a manifestation of the then inherently expedient mode of product uniting was a direct output expression of input availabilities based on the static externalized unity-package mould images that swept out in purely horizontal developing responses to world hamburger demand transitions.

In 1927 I was attempting to offset the inherent inertia of a silicone vesselized package-unit of Heinz catsup by the then omni-accepted thrust-energizing squirt-out method. I saw quite clearly that an extraordinary pounds-per-bottom thrust impulse was required in ever-increasing impulse frequency in order to produce a required catsup layering pattern on the previously steam-activated hot dog I had decided to eat.

Extrapolating from the non-layering catsup event sequence poundings to an event-anticipating system requiring perhaps far fewer p.p.b.i.'s, it occurred to me that within the vast inventory of industrial systems as yet uncatalyzed from the purely local-event oriented but immeasurably more sophisticated demands of the Boer War to serve the growing tomatoing demands of world population, there should exist a sub-systeming capability that could accomodate both man's gustatory sweep-out and his reduced Time threshold frequency.

Long before, I had seen that the black-
smiths and iron-mongerers excited the heat-
energy slaving potential of their horse shoe-
ing flame-ins by introducing a massive oxygen
recycling pattern through the man-controlled
push-pull of a volume-forwarding device called
a bellows.

This bellowsing capability thus employed
in the smithy-focussed environment-demand en-
abled him, quite easily, to transform the progressively softening metals of his local trad-
ing into progressively sophisticated programs
for ever outward-sweeping interconnections with
his Earth environments.

It then became excitingly apparent to me
that this sequential jet-thrust capability en-
gendered by man's bellows could be re-invested
in an entire new spectrum range of activities
including his package-uniting.

My initial exploration into bellows cat-
supry were forcefully implemented by world
physicians in a spontaneous expansion of their
curingry inventory. The bellowsing proclivity
of the hypodermic syringe was in modest anti-
cipation of such pattern spanning life orienta-
tions as tetracycline and atabrine.

The total hitting power of man's expres-
sible bellowsing has now been synergized in
the total range performance capability net-
working of our historically jug-locked unit
packaging inadequacies. We see quite clearly
that the polyethyl packaging systems with
throwaway alternative build-in have transform-
ed the entire funded technology of catsup package unitizing into an immediate man-advantage
bearing consequentially upon his time-resource
availability and energy loading potential.

                        Pete Brown, 1966, with
                        apologies to Bucky

37

PESTO SAUCE

3 cups packed fresh basil leaves
2 cloves garlic, chopped
¼ cup pine nuts
¼ cup butter
¼ cup olive oil
½ cup grated parmesan
salt to taste
(2 lbs. spaghetti)

Put basil, garlic, pine nuts, butter, oil,
parmesan together in blender. Puree until
smooth. Mix in with 2 lbs. cooked spaghetti
for spaghetti al pesto. Also can be used as
dressing for baked potatoes, potato salad,
filling for omelettes, and tortellini salad,
etc.

Amy Edmondson

TORTELLINI SALAD

1 16 oz. pkg. tortellini
½ cup pesto sauce
½ cup minced italian pimentos
½ cup olive oil
juice of one lemon
salt and pepper
¼ cup garlic vinegar*

Boil tortellini in salted water until soft
and done. Drain and place in bowl. Add
pesto sauce, pimentos, olive oil, lemon juice,
salt and pepper, and garlic vinegar. Chill
and serve. Makes 6-8 servings.

*To make garlic vinegar, slice garlic cloves,
one per cup of vinegar, combine the two ingredients, and let sit in cabinet for two weeks,
the longer it soaks, the more flavorful the
vinegar becomes.

Elizabeth Choy

ENTREES

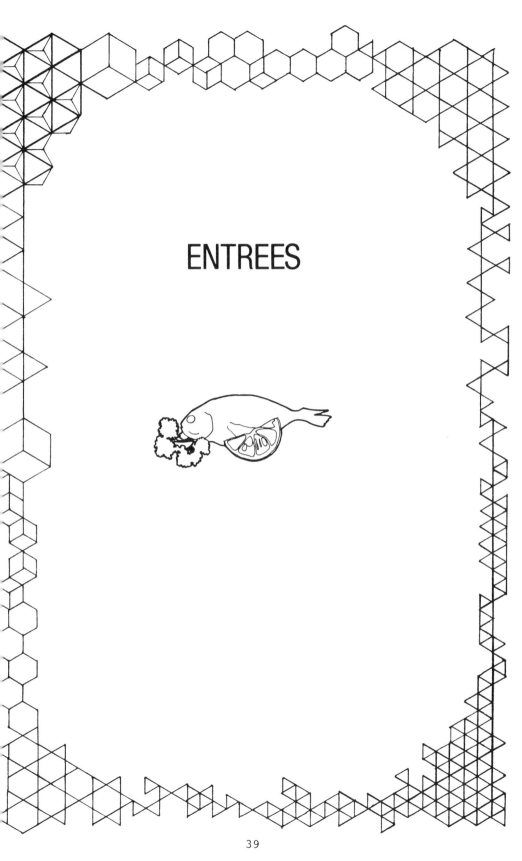

DYMAXION CARP

Carp is not usually thought of as a fine eating fish, but when caught in very fresh water, far from civilization, and cooked on the spot, can be an unusual and excellent experience in Dymaxion dining. This recipe was developed, with the help of a pair of Shoshone Indians and members of the Rainbow Family, in the Wind River Wilderness Area of Wyoming.

1 2-3 lb. freshly caught and cleaned carp (or other fleshy and sizable fish)
1 handful of freshly gathered herbs (for example, crushed watercress and sage)
1 tsp. Dr. Bronner's Mineral Salt
  additional salt and pepper to taste

Prepare campfire with hardwoods until coals are glowing and the flames have died down. Wrap the herbed and seasoned fish carefully in aluminum foil with a handful of water if needed. Bury in the coals for about 30 minutes. Check for doneness. Eat while still hot.

Kiyoshi Kuromiya

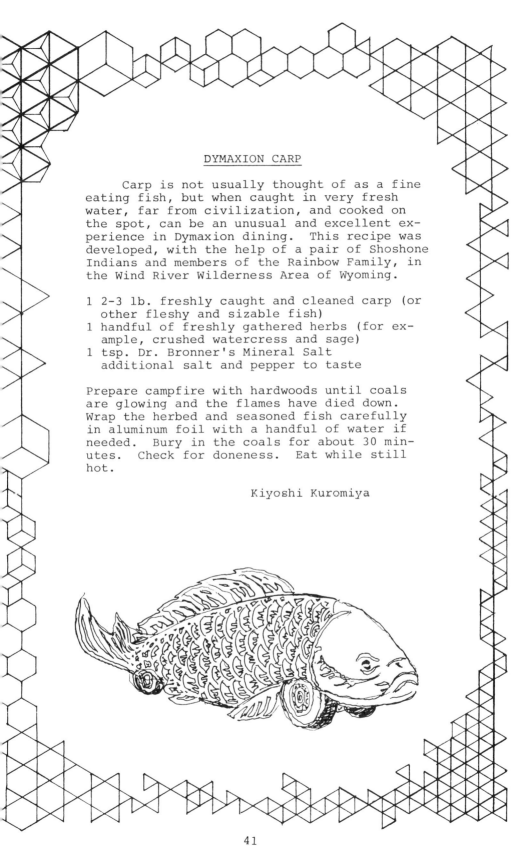

41

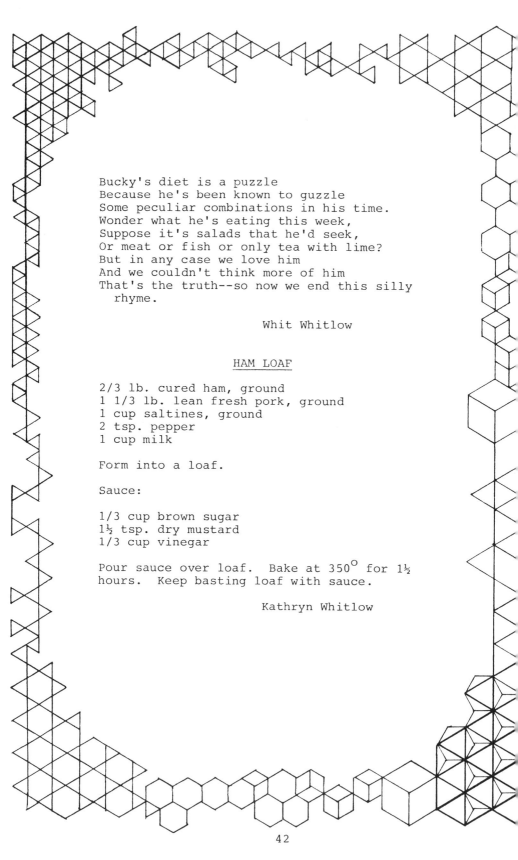

Bucky's diet is a puzzle
Because he's been known to guzzle
Some peculiar combinations in his time.
Wonder what he's eating this week,
Suppose it's salads that he'd seek,
Or meat or fish or only tea with lime?
But in any case we love him
And we couldn't think more of him
That's the truth--so now we end this silly
  rhyme.

Whit Whitlow

HAM LOAF

2/3 lb. cured ham, ground
1 1/3 lb. lean fresh pork, ground
1 cup saltines, ground
2 tsp. pepper
1 cup milk

Form into a loaf.

Sauce:

1/3 cup brown sugar
1½ tsp. dry mustard
1/3 cup vinegar

Pour sauce over loaf. Bake at 350° for 1½
hours. Keep basting loaf with sauce.

Kathryn Whitlow

RUSSIAN HUNTER'S STEW

1 lb. lean bacon, cut in 1½" squares
1 lb. any cheap cut (e.g. shoulder), in
   similar squares
1 lb. Russian hunter's sausage, sliced in 1"
   bits (substitute Polish hard sausage if Russian is not available)
8 medium size white onions (or yellow)
6 winter carrots sliced in hunks
6 good sized turnips, cut in squares
2 winter celery roots, cut in pieces
6 medium sized potatoes, peeled and halved
½ hard white winter cabbage, cut, not diced
dill
salt, pepper, paprika
sour cream

Put the bacon and beef in ample pot with sufficient water to simmer gently. Put pot on
back of stove, Russian wood-burning stove or
campfire preferable. After a couple of hours,
add winter carrots, turnip, onions, sausage.
An hour later add potatoes, celery roots.
Season to taste and add sufficient water occasionally, to cover stew. Allow three to
four hours for cooking, the slower the better.
In Russia, the stew would simmer all day on
the back of the stove. When ready to serve
sprinkle with chopped dill and add a generous
dob of sour cream to each portion. This
should be plenty for four people and some left
over. As you can see, the proportions are
very flexible, but the net result is dandy.

                              Harrison Salisbury

43

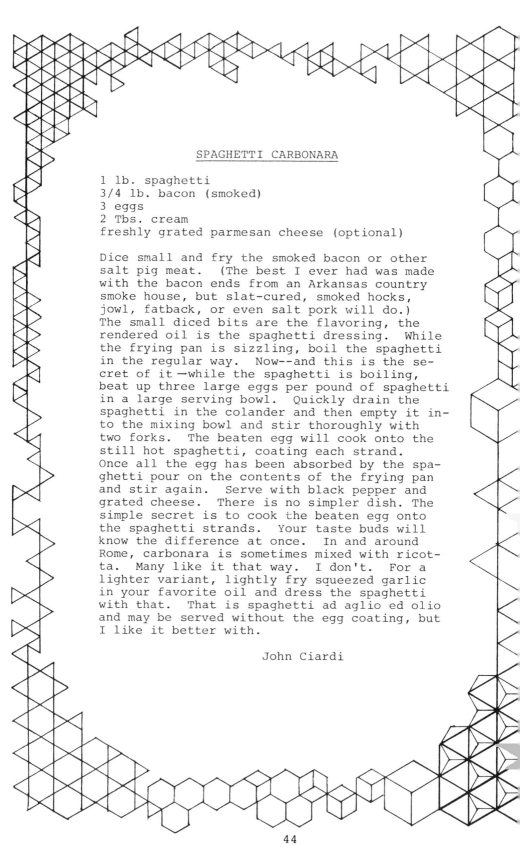

SPAGHETTI CARBONARA

1 lb. spaghetti
3/4 lb. bacon (smoked)
3 eggs
2 Tbs. cream
freshly grated parmesan cheese (optional)

Dice small and fry the smoked bacon or other
salt pig meat. (The best I ever had was made
with the bacon ends from an Arkansas country
smoke house, but slat-cured, smoked hocks,
jowl, fatback, or even salt pork will do.)
The small diced bits are the flavoring, the
rendered oil is the spaghetti dressing. While
the frying pan is sizzling, boil the spaghetti
in the regular way. Now--and this is the secret of it —while the spaghetti is boiling,
beat up three large eggs per pound of spaghetti
in a large serving bowl. Quickly drain the
spaghetti in the colander and then empty it into the mixing bowl and stir thoroughly with
two forks. The beaten egg will cook onto the
still hot spaghetti, coating each strand.
Once all the egg has been absorbed by the spaghetti pour on the contents of the frying pan
and stir again. Serve with black pepper and
grated cheese. There is no simpler dish. The
simple secret is to cook the beaten egg onto
the spaghetti strands. Your taste buds will
know the difference at once. In and around
Rome, carbonara is sometimes mixed with ricot-
ta. Many like it that way. I don't. For a
lighter variant, lightly fry squeezed garlic
in your favorite oil and dress the spaghetti
with that. That is spaghetti ad aglio ed olio
and may be served without the egg coating, but
I like it better with.

John Ciardi

STUFFED AUBERGINES

4 large aubergines
2 onions, finely chopped
2 cloves crushed garlic
4-6 oz. thinly sliced fresh mushrooms
4 large ripe red tomatoes, skinned, seeded,
  and chopped
1 Tbs. tomato puree
a few stoned black olives
3 oz. brown breadcrumbs
3 oz. grated gruyere cheese
½ pt. stock
5-6 chopped anchovy fillets
2 Tbs. chopped parsley
marjoram, thyme, oregano

Cut the aubergines in half lengthwise; scoop
out the pulp leaving the shells intact. Salt
and drain the shells for about 30 minutes,
then rinse and dry carefully. Fry the onions,
aubergine pulp, and mushrooms gently in some
butter until very soft. Add the tomato puree,
herbs, garlic, and stock, stirring well, and
finally the anchovies and olives. Mix the
breadcrumbs, cheese, and parsley, and add the
cooked tomato mixture to them. Paint the skin
of each halved aubergine with olive oil, and
pile the mixture into each half. Bake in a
covered dish in a moderate oven until the
shells have softened and are cooked through.

Yehudi Menuhin

45

Fuller's staple, or at least his preferred diet at every meal, is steak, a diet that
helps him keep his weight trim, suppress a ten-
dency to diverticulitis, and above all refuel
those enormous stores of energy. His rate of
metabolism would be the envy of a shrew. When
young vegetarians express dismay at his beef-
eating vice--it does not conform to their idea
of his persona--he has to explain that the
cows are eating much more vegetation and converting it to protein than he could possibly
cope with first hand.

> Ed Applewhite,
> COSMIC FISHING

Dr. Mead did very little cooking, but
she did enjoy preparing a few dishes. This
was a favorite.

STEAK AND MUSHROOMS WITH LEMON

2 lbs. sirloin steak, 1½" thick
1 lb. fresh mushrooms
1 lemon
salt and pepper

Cook favorite cut of steak to desired doneness. Saute mushrooms in butter, add salt and
pepper, squeeze juice of lemon over mushrooms
after mushrooms are cooked, stir gently.
Serve mushrooms poured over steak and enjoy a
most delicious and unusual flavor.

> Margaret Mead

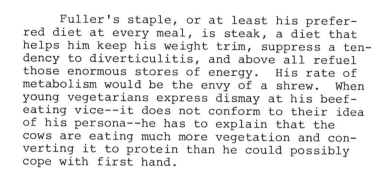

BAKED CHICKEN

1 chicken
2 Tbs. salt
¼ tsp. black pepper
3 cloves grated garlic
1 Tbs. fresh grated ginger

Wash chicken, remove fat, drain. Combine
salt, pepper, garlic, and ginger. Rub chick-
en with the mixture. Let stand for 4-5 hours.
Put chicken into uncovered iron pot. Turn on
oven, bake for 40 minutes at 500°. Without
opening, turn oven off and let chicken continue to bake until done (total time approximately 1 hour). It can remain in the oven until
ready to serve.

It is very attractive deboned and sliced into
3/4" - 1" pieces. Garnish with chinese chives
or cilantro. Serve with rice and salad.

Mae Lee

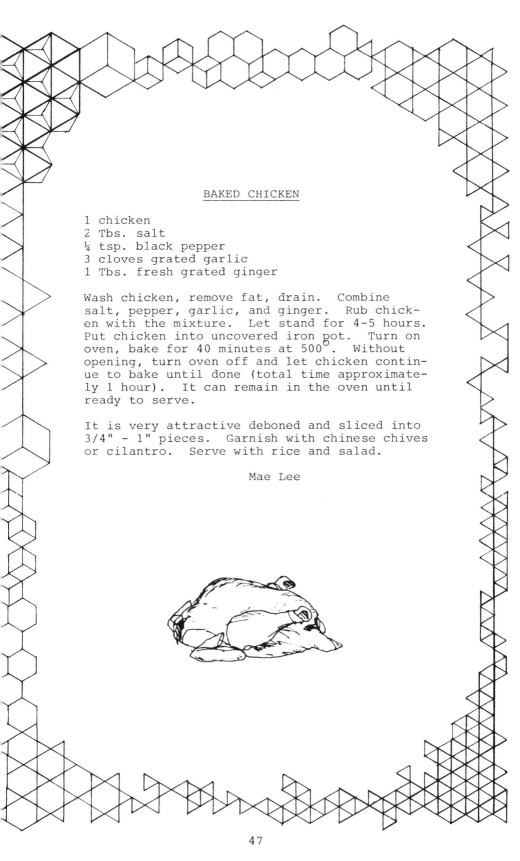

47

Maine innkeepers George and Eleanor Pavloff, of the Goose Cove Lodge on Deer Isle,
serve wonderful food in great style to Bucky
and his guests. We received the following
from Eleanor Pavloff:

"When Bucky comes to Goose Cove Lodge for
dinner, I usually serve him chicken or fish.
The following recipe is a favorite of his and
involves the use of lemon comfit."

A PILGRIM'S CHICKEN

Serves 6 to 8

8 boneless chicken breasts
1 pickled lemon (see lemon comfit recipe)
1 small onion
1 clove garlic
1 cup dry vermouth or white wine
½ pint sour cream
pepper
paprika (sweet Hungarian is preferred)

Chop one pickled lemon, onion, and garlic in
food processor. Rub chicken breasts with half
of mixture. Pepper. Brown lightly in olive
oil. Pour off excess oil and deglaze pan with
½ cup wine. Arrange on baking dish (I use a
low sided casserole), pour deglazed pan juices
over chicken. Spread remaining lemon comfit
mixture over chicken breasts. Spread sour
cream, mixed with remaining wine, over chicken.
Sprinkle with paprika. Bake in 350° oven for
40 minutes. Serve on platter in bed of rice.

Eleanor Pavloff

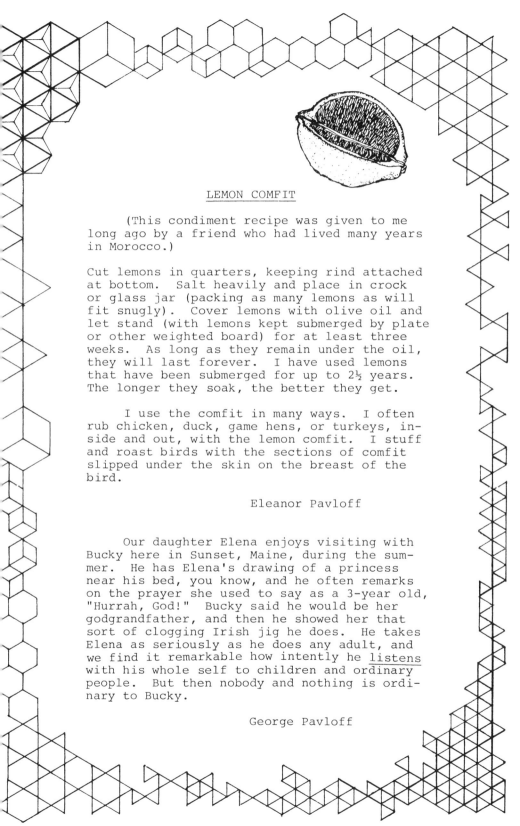

LEMON COMFIT

(This condiment recipe was given to me long ago by a friend who had lived many years in Morocco.)

Cut lemons in quarters, keeping rind attached at bottom. Salt heavily and place in crock or glass jar (packing as many lemons as will fit snugly). Cover lemons with olive oil and let stand (with lemons kept submerged by plate or other weighted board) for at least three weeks. As long as they remain under the oil, they will last forever. I have used lemons that have been submerged for up to 2½ years. The longer they soak, the better they get.

I use the comfit in many ways. I often rub chicken, duck, game hens, or turkeys, inside and out, with the lemon comfit. I stuff and roast birds with the sections of comfit slipped under the skin on the breast of the bird.

Eleanor Pavloff

Our daughter Elena enjoys visiting with Bucky here in Sunset, Maine, during the summer. He has Elena's drawing of a princess near his bed, you know, and he often remarks on the prayer she used to say as a 3-year old, "Hurrah, God!" Bucky said he would be her godgrandfather, and then he showed her that sort of clogging Irish jig he does. He takes Elena as seriously as he does any adult, and we find it remarkable how intently he listens with his whole self to children and ordinary people. But then nobody and nothing is ordinary to Bucky.

George Pavloff

Elena Pavloff

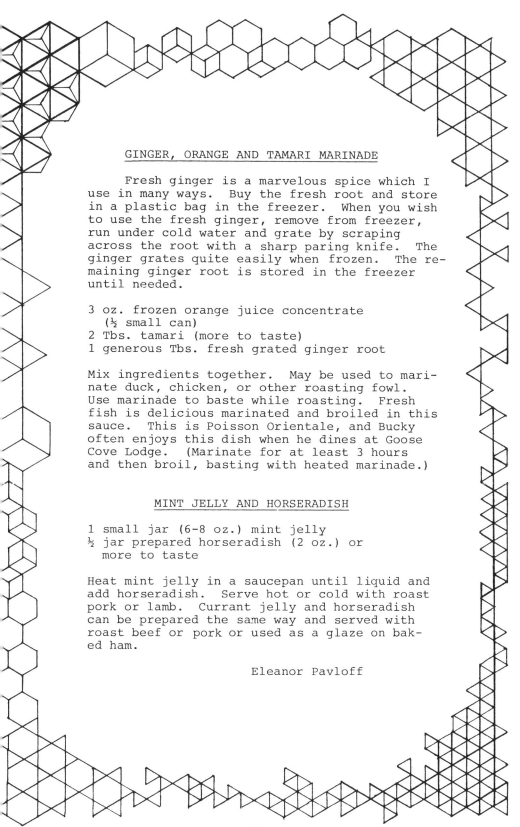

GINGER, ORANGE AND TAMARI MARINADE

Fresh ginger is a marvelous spice which I use in many ways. Buy the fresh root and store in a plastic bag in the freezer. When you wish to use the fresh ginger, remove from freezer, run under cold water and grate by scraping across the root with a sharp paring knife. The ginger grates quite easily when frozen. The remaining ginger root is stored in the freezer until needed.

3 oz. frozen orange juice concentrate
  (½ small can)
2 Tbs. tamari (more to taste)
1 generous Tbs. fresh grated ginger root

Mix ingredients together. May be used to marinate duck, chicken, or other roasting fowl. Use marinade to baste while roasting. Fresh fish is delicious marinated and broiled in this sauce. This is Poisson Orientale, and Bucky often enjoys this dish when he dines at Goose Cove Lodge. (Marinate for at least 3 hours and then broil, basting with heated marinade.)

MINT JELLY AND HORSERADISH

1 small jar (6-8 oz.) mint jelly
½ jar prepared horseradish (2 oz.) or
  more to taste

Heat mint jelly in a saucepan until liquid and add horseradish. Serve hot or cold with roast pork or lamb. Currant jelly and horseradish can be prepared the same way and served with roast beef or pork or used as a glaze on baked ham.

Eleanor Pavloff

GILDING THE LILY

1. Towards the end of roasting a rib of beef, brush all the fat with a paste of dry mustard powder and soy sauce.

2. To roast a grouse: leave the heart and liver in the bird. Roast with a bacon cover as is done normally. Finally, baste thoroughly with the liquor from inside the bird.

   Sounds disgusting, doesn't it? It's actually very good.

3. Whilst grilling cheese on toast, add dry grated horseradish, Worcestershire sauce, and a pinch of sweet basil.

                        Cedric Price

SATE LILEH (BALI)
BROILED SKEWERED FISH STICKS

To make 8 sate

3 Tbs. vegetable oil
2 Tbs. finely chopped onions
½ tsp. finely chopped garlic
A 2 to 2½ lb. pike or other firm, white-flesh-
   ed fish, cleaned, skinned, boned, and finely ground (about 1 cup ground)
2 Tbs. rich coconut top milk
¼ tsp. strained fresh lime juice
½ tsp. salt
1/8 tsp. white pepper

In a heavy 6" to 8" skillet, heat 1 tablespoon of the oil over moderate heat until a light haze forms above it. Drop in the onions and garlic and, stirring frequently, cook for 4 or 5 minutes until they are soft and trans-

parent, but not brown. Watch carefully for
any sign of burning and regulate the heat ac-
cordingly. Transfer the entire contents of
the skillet to a deep bowl and add the fish,
coconut milk, lime juice, salt and white pepper. Beat vigorously with a spoon until the
mixture is smooth, then cover tightly and
marinate in the refrigerator for at least 1
hour. Light a layer of coals in a charcoal
broiler or hibachi and let them burn until a
white ash appears on the surface, or preheat
the broiler of your range to its highest
point. With a pastry brush, spread vegetable
oil evenly on both sides of eight ¼" wide,
flat stainless steel skewers, about 10" long.
Divide the fish mixture into 8 portions and
shape them into small cylinders. Thread each
cylinder on a separate skewer, further patting
the fish into a smooth, somewhat flattened
sausage shape about 3½" to 4" long. Brush
about 1 tablespoon of vegetable oil evenly
over the grill of the charcoal broiler or hibachi, or on the rack of the broiler pan. Arrange the sate on the grill or rack and broil
them 4" from the heat for 3 minutes. Brush
the sate lightly with the remaining oil and
using a metal spatula, gently turn them over.
Broil for 3 minutes more, or until they are
firm and delicately browned. Serve at once.

Steve Parker

SHRIMP FILÉ GUMBO
From the Louisiana Kid

Serves 8 or more

Roux:

2/3 cup oil
2/3 cup flour

Gumbo Base:

2 cups chopped onion
1 cup chopped green pepper
½ cup thinly sliced scallion tops
1 Tbs. minced garlic
2 Tbs. finely minced parsley
1 lb. smoked sausage, sliced in ½" pieces
3 lbs. chicken pieces
2 lbs. whole shrimp, peeled and deveined
1 lb. lump crabmeat

Liquid and Seasonings:

2 qts. cold water
2 tsp. salt (to taste)
1½ tsp. black pepper
¼ tsp. cayenne
1 tsp. dried thyme
1 tsp. dried basil
3 whole bay leaves
3 Tbs. filé powder

Prepare ingredients for gumbo base. Heat oil
in large heavy pot over high heat. Brown
chicken parts in hot oil. Remove to platter
and keep warm. Prepare roux by adding flour
to oil, stirring continually until dark brown.
Add sausage, onion, peppers, scallions, and
garlic, and cook over medium low heat for approximately 15 minutes. Add 1 cup of the
water, the browned chicken parts, and all sea-

sonings except the filé powder. Mix gently
but thoroughly. Gradually add remaining water
and bring to a boil at medium heat. Reduce
heat to low and simmer for ½ hour. Add crabmeat, and simmer for another ½ hour to 45 minutes. Add shrimp to gumbo, and cook approximately 10 minutes. Remove pot from heat, add
filé powder, and allow to sit for 10 minutes.
Serve in bowls over boiled white rice.

Peter Simoneaux

COLUMBIAN TAMALES

4 cups fine corn meal
3 to 3½ Tbs. cumin
2 pork chops
2 chicken breasts
½ cup Spanish olives
½ cup capers
3 Tbs. olive oil
2 cups water

Dice and fry the pork, set aside, and debone
the chicken, and cook it similarly. Mix all
ingredients in a bowl, and adjust the water,
adding enough to make a very thick paste.
Add the diced and fried chicken and pork.
Take a large piece of aluminum foil, and put
about a cup of the mixture on it. Form the
paste into a small loaf, and wrap the aluminum foil around it. Tie the flat loaf with
kitchen string, like a package, wrapping the
string lengthwise and across about three or
four times, and then knot it. Do the same
with the rest of the paste. You should have
four tamales. Steam them in the foil for 45
minutes, or until set. Unwrap, and serve with
stewed tomatoes and salad.

Elizabeth Choy

THE RIGHT DINNER

In the late summer of 1980, Bucky, Shirley Sharkey and I were in Sophia, Bulgaria, for a series of high-powered meetings with heads of state arranged by Cleveland industrialist Cyrus Eaton, Jr., who, with his staff, was traveling with us. During our stay in Bulgaria, a member of the Eastern European Communist Federation, we were always shadowed by men dressed, appropriately enough, in black turtlenecks. Guides, we were told, as well as bodyguards, although they didn't speak any English.

The meetings were successful, and to cap them off, the government dignitaries wanted to give a big dinner, a banquet at a small mountain called de Luna, at a new hotel they wanted to show off. A limousine would call at our hotel at 8:00 PM.

To our pleased surprise, a sleek new Mercedes limousine appeared to take the three of us to dinner. (Cyrus Eaton had left earlier, planning to meet us there.) I tried to communicate, to make sure we were getting in the right car. WE ARE GOING TO DE LUNA. HE (pointing to Bucky) BUCKY FULLER. OK? FULLER MAKES DOMES. ROUND BUILDINGS. OK?

Blank expressions. The "guides" shrugged their shoulders. We realized that it was definitely a different driver. And the "guides" had changed their costumes--at least, their turtlenecks were a different color. Baffling. DE LUNA? The guides shook their heads, mumbling "Otani." Worried consultation with Shirley. De Luna, right? Look, I wrote it down.

56

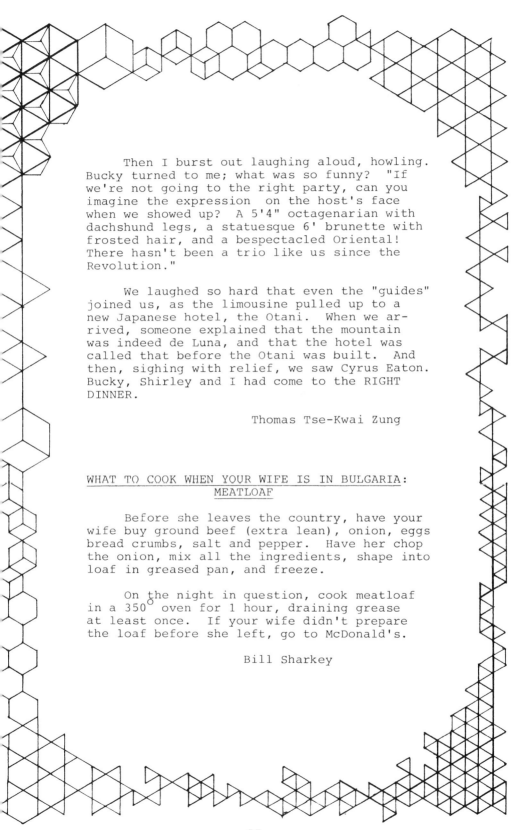

Then I burst out laughing aloud, howling. Bucky turned to me; what was so funny? "If we're not going to the right party, can you imagine the expression on the host's face when we showed up? A 5'4" octagenarian with dachshund legs, a statuesque 6' brunette with frosted hair, and a bespectacled Oriental! There hasn't been a trio like us since the Revolution."

We laughed so hard that even the "guides" joined us, as the limousine pulled up to a new Japanese hotel, the Otani. When we arrived, someone explained that the mountain was indeed de Luna, and that the hotel was called that before the Otani was built. And then, sighing with relief, we saw Cyrus Eaton. Bucky, Shirley and I had come to the RIGHT DINNER.

Thomas Tse-Kwai Zung

WHAT TO COOK WHEN YOUR WIFE IS IN BULGARIA: MEATLOAF

Before she leaves the country, have your wife buy ground beef (extra lean), onion, eggs bread crumbs, salt and pepper. Have her chop the onion, mix all the ingredients, shape into loaf in greased pan, and freeze.

On the night in question, cook meatloaf in a 350° oven for 1 hour, draining grease at least once. If your wife didn't prepare the loaf before she left, go to McDonald's.

Bill Sharkey

ROCK CORNISH GAME HENS IN CREAM

4 Rock Cornish Game Hens
2 cups light cream
½ cup flour
½ tsp. salt
¼ tsp. black pepper
pinch nutmeg

¼ tsp. cloves
¼ tsp. thyme
4 juniper berries,
　crushed
¼ cup olive oil
4 slices white bread
　toasted
red currant jelly

Disjoint hens into 4 pieces each--two breasts,
two leg and thigh pieces. Marinate in
cream for one hour. Combine flour with all
spices and herbs. Remove hens from cream,
roll in seasoned flour and saute in olive oil
until browned on both sides and cooked through
(about ½ hour). Serve on toast which has been
spread with red currant jelly and top with
cream sauce.

Cream sauce:

2 Tbs. flour
2 Tbs. butter
2 Tbs. madeira
1 cup light cream used to marinate hens

Melt butter in a heavy pan and add flour.
Cook gently for 3 minutes. Add cream and stir
constantly over low flame until sauce has
thickened. Add madeira, salt and pepper to
taste, and pour over hens on toast.

Ann Mintz

INCHE KABIN

1 fresh chicken, about 3 3/4 lbs.
4 shallots
4 fresh red chilis
3/4 oz. turmeric powder
3/4 oz. curry powder
1/3 cup thick coconut milk
salt to taste
freshly ground black pepper
oil for deep frying
prawn crackers

Prepare the chicken and cut into pieces.
Finely chop the shallots and chilis and pound
together with the turmeric and curry powder.
Place the spice paste in a large dish, add the
coconut milk, season with salt and freshly
ground black pepper and stir to blend thoroughly. Place the chicken pieces in the dish
and set aside in a cool place to marinate for
1 hour. Heat the oil in a large pan until almost smoking, then remove the chicken from the
marinade and place immediately into the hot
oil. Fry until 3/4 cooked, then remove, drain,
and replace in the oil to cook until tender,
crispy, and golden. Serve with prawn crackers
and a sauce dip, recipe below. Serves 4 to 6.

2 shallots
2 fresh red chilis
1 stalk lemon grass
2 tsp. fresh lime juice
2 tsp. sugar
2 tsp. English mustard powder
2 Tbs. light soya sauce
1/3 cup Worcestershire sauce

To make the sauce, chop the shallots, chilis,
and lemon grass very finely and mix with the
lime juice, sugar, English mustard, soya sauce,
and Worcestershire sauce. Stir until the
sugar and mustard are completely dissolved.

Lim Chong Keat

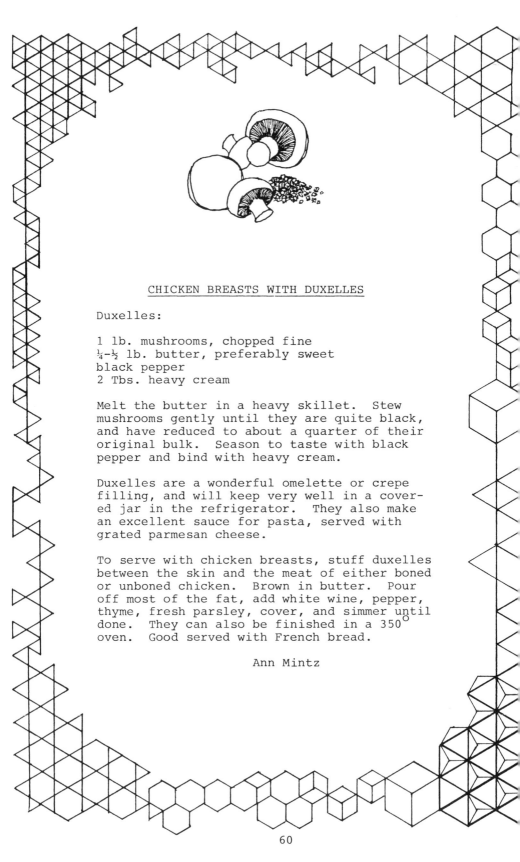

CHICKEN BREASTS WITH DUXELLES

Duxelles:

1 lb. mushrooms, chopped fine
¼-½ lb. butter, preferably sweet
black pepper
2 Tbs. heavy cream

Melt the butter in a heavy skillet. Stew
mushrooms gently until they are quite black,
and have reduced to about a quarter of their
original bulk. Season to taste with black
pepper and bind with heavy cream.

Duxelles are a wonderful omelette or crepe
filling, and will keep very well in a covered jar in the refrigerator. They also make
an excellent sauce for pasta, served with
grated parmesan cheese.

To serve with chicken breasts, stuff duxelles
between the skin and the meat of either boned
or unboned chicken. Brown in butter. Pour
off most of the fat, add white wine, pepper,
thyme, fresh parsley, cover, and simmer until
done. They can also be finished in a 350°
oven. Good served with French bread.

Ann Mintz

BREADSTUFFS

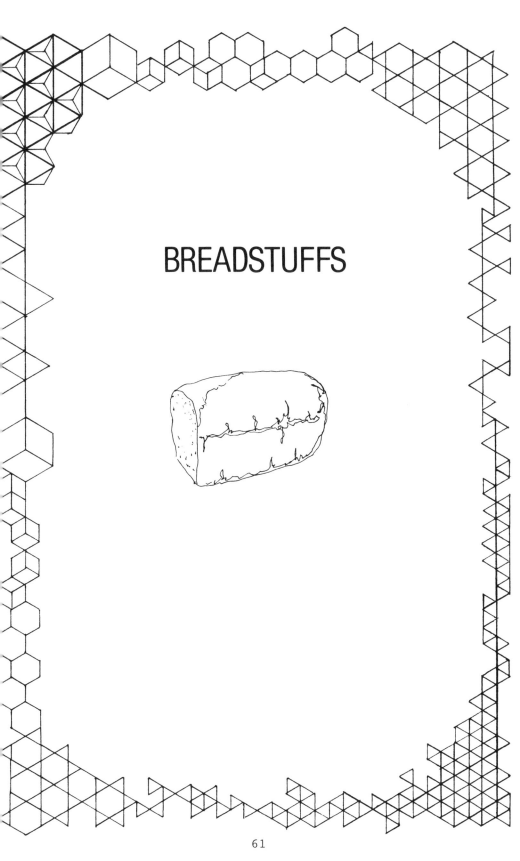

SPOON BREAD

3/4 cup hominy grits, or quick cooking grits
1 cup boiling water
2 cups milk
2 Tbs. sugar
pinch of salt
2 Tbs. butter
1 beaten egg

Mix grits with water. Add one cup milk, sugar,
salt. Cook in a double boiler for ½ hour.
Add butter. Add other cup of milk. Cook.
Add one beaten egg. Put in buttered dish.
Bake 10 minutes at 400°, then 50 minutes at
350° Sprinkle with cinnamon.

Gerard K. O'Neill

PUMPKIN BREAD

2/3 cup butter   1½ tsp. salt
2 2/3 cups sugar   ½ tsp. baking powder
4 eggs   1 tsp. cinnamon
1 lb. canned pumpkin   1 tsp. cloves
2/3 cup water   2/3 cup nuts
2 1/3 cup flour   2/3 cup raisins
2 tsp. baking soda

Grease 2 loaf pans. Cream butter and sugar
until fluffy. Stir in eggs, pumpkin, water.
Blend in flour, soda, salt, baking powder,
cinnamon, cloves--stir in raisins and nuts.
Pour into pans. Bake at 350° about 70 minutes, until toothpick comes out dry.

Shirley Sharkey

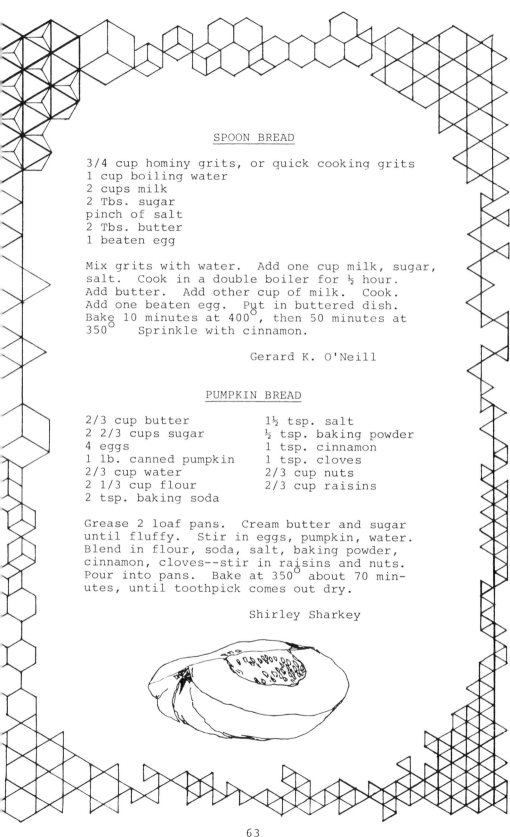

63

PANCAKES

2 cups sweet rice flour
1 cup cornmeal
3 tsp. baking powder
1 scant tsp. salt
3 Tbs. oil
½ cup tofu
2 cups (approximately) water

Combine dry ingredients; blend or whip together oil, tofu, and water. Add to dry ingredients (you may need more water). Mix together. Fry in dry frying pan over medium
high heat. Start heating pan after you've
got dry ingredients together so that it will
be hot enough when you start. Add fruit to
the batter if you feel like it--raspberries,
strawberries, blueberries, apples, or peaches.

Serve with tahini and maple syrup.

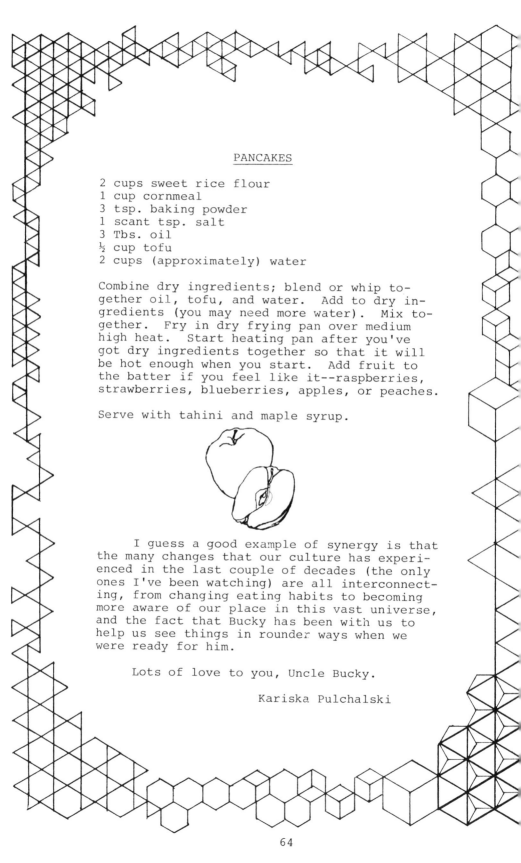

I guess a good example of synergy is that
the many changes that our culture has experienced in the last couple of decades (the only
ones I've been watching) are all interconnect-
ing, from changing eating habits to becoming
more aware of our place in this vast universe,
and the fact that Bucky has been with us to
help us see things in rounder ways when we
were ready for him.

Lots of love to you, Uncle Bucky.

Kariska Pulchalski

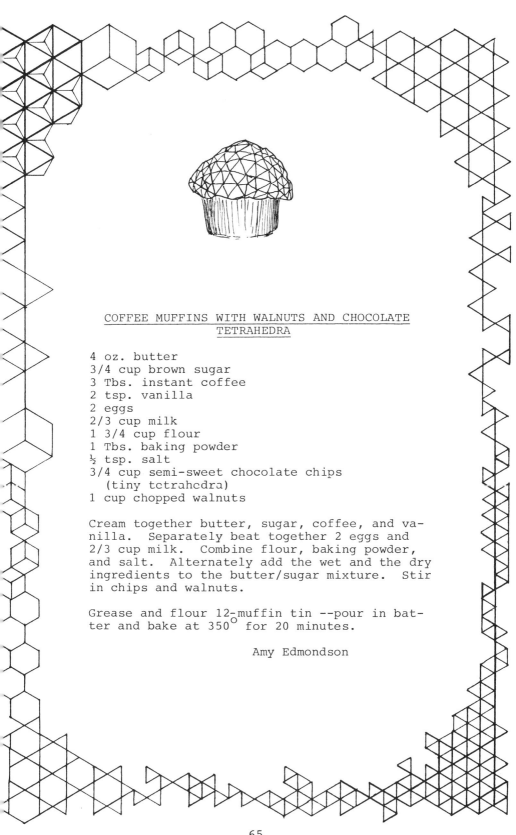

COFFEE MUFFINS WITH WALNUTS AND CHOCOLATE
TETRAHEDRA

4 oz. butter
3/4 cup brown sugar
3 Tbs. instant coffee
2 tsp. vanilla
2 eggs
2/3 cup milk
1 3/4 cup flour
1 Tbs. baking powder
½ tsp. salt
3/4 cup semi-sweet chocolate chips
  (tiny tctrahcdra)
1 cup chopped walnuts

Cream together butter, sugar, coffee, and vanilla. Separately beat together 2 eggs and
2/3 cup milk. Combine flour, baking powder,
and salt. Alternately add the wet and the dry
ingredients to the butter/sugar mixture. Stir
in chips and walnuts.

Grease and flour 12-muffin tin --pour in batter and bake at 350° for 20 minutes.

Amy Edmondson

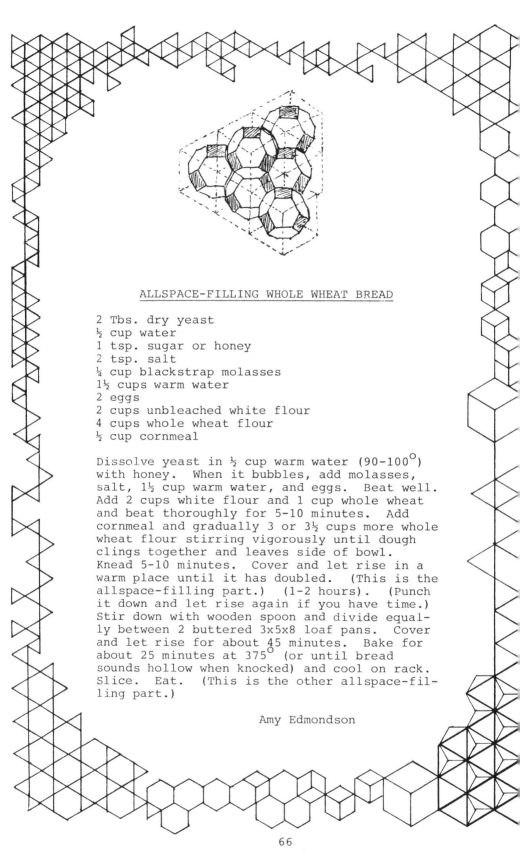

ALLSPACE-FILLING WHOLE WHEAT BREAD

2 Tbs. dry yeast
½ cup water
1 tsp. sugar or honey
2 tsp. salt
¼ cup blackstrap molasses
1½ cups warm water
2 eggs
2 cups unbleached white flour
4 cups whole wheat flour
½ cup cornmeal

Dissolve yeast in ½ cup warm water ($90-100^{\circ}$)
with honey. When it bubbles, add molasses,
salt, 1½ cup warm water, and eggs. Beat well.
Add 2 cups white flour and 1 cup whole wheat
and beat thoroughly for 5-10 minutes. Add
cornmeal and gradually 3 or 3½ cups more whole
wheat flour stirring vigorously until dough
clings together and leaves side of bowl.
Knead 5-10 minutes. Cover and let rise in a
warm place until it has doubled. (This is the
allspace-filling part.) (1-2 hours). (Punch
it down and let rise again if you have time.)
Stir down with wooden spoon and divide equal-
ly between 2 buttered 3x5x8 loaf pans. Cover
and let rise for about 45 minutes. Bake for
about 25 minutes at 375° (or until bread
sounds hollow when knocked) and cool on rack.
Slice. Eat. (This is the other allspace-filling part.)

                    Amy Edmondson

I first met Buckminster Fuller about four
years ago. A colleague in the Institute for
Scientific Information had told me that he
needed a new office. Since ISI was planning
our new building at the time, it was suggested that Bucky could use space on the fourth
floor of our building. A meeting was arranged
to discuss this and to get better acquainted.
I remember my first impression of Bucky. He
seemed like an elf, small, quiet, and frequently smiling. After a brief negotiation, he
moved into our building. It is a pleasure for
me to tell visitors that such a distinguished
scholar has his professional residence here.
I only wish that he stayed around more often;
he travels more than I do.

When I first met Bucky, he told me that
he was born hyperopic or far-sighted, but his
eyes were not corrected with glasses until he
was four years old. Until then, he says, he
had never seen the details of objects, only
their outlines and general shapes. Through-
out his life, he has retained a penchant for
concentrating on the large shapes around him
rather than the details.

Despite his age--he recently turned 87--
Bucky is still going strong. His staff keeps
busy handling a full schedule of trips,
speeches, artifact development, and publication. He has done much toward ensuring us a
comfortable future on this planet by insist-
ing that we plan for the future and by his
insistence that we unite as a planet of people. In his own way, Bucky has spent his life-
time as an ambassador of peace.

from "A Tribute to Buck-
minster Fuller" by
Eugene Garfield

ONION RYE BREAD

2 Tbs. dry yeast
1½ cups warm water
¼ cup molasses
3 tsp. salt
3 cups rye flour
3 cups unbleached white flour
1 Tbs. caraway seeds
1 small chopped onion

Sprinkle yeast over warm water and let sit for
10 minutes until bubbly. Then add molasses,
salt, and the rye flour, 1 cup at a time, stirring well after each addition. Add unbleached
white flour, 1 cup at a time, stirring well
until dough leaves sides of bowl and is ready
for kneading. Then add the caraway seeds and
the onion, kneading them into the dough. On
floured surface, knead dough well for 10-15
minutes, then put in greased bowl, cover and
let rise for 1 or 2 hours until doubled.
Punch down, separate into 2 loaves, put in
greased 3x5x8 bread pans, cover and let rise
again, 45-60 minutes, and then bake at 375°
for 30-40 minutes, until loaves sound hollow
when knocked. Good served hot with cream
cheese.

Amy Edmondson

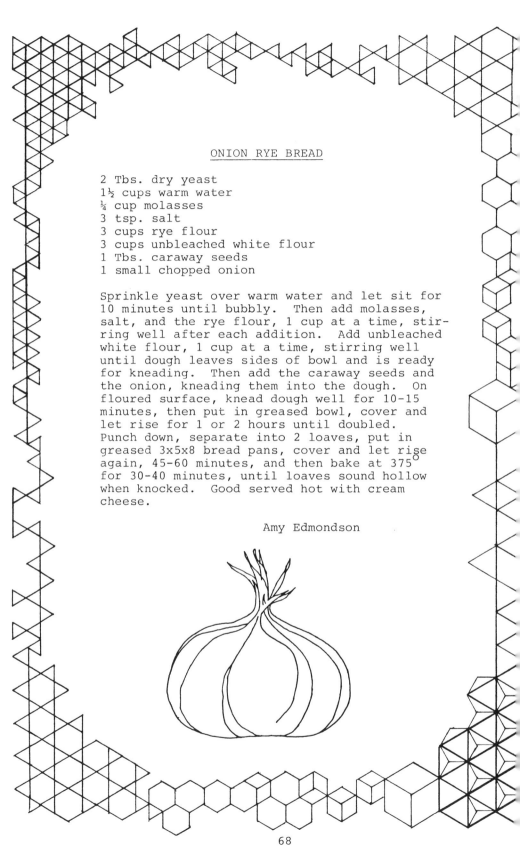

A MACROBIOTIC DIET

BY JOHN CAGE

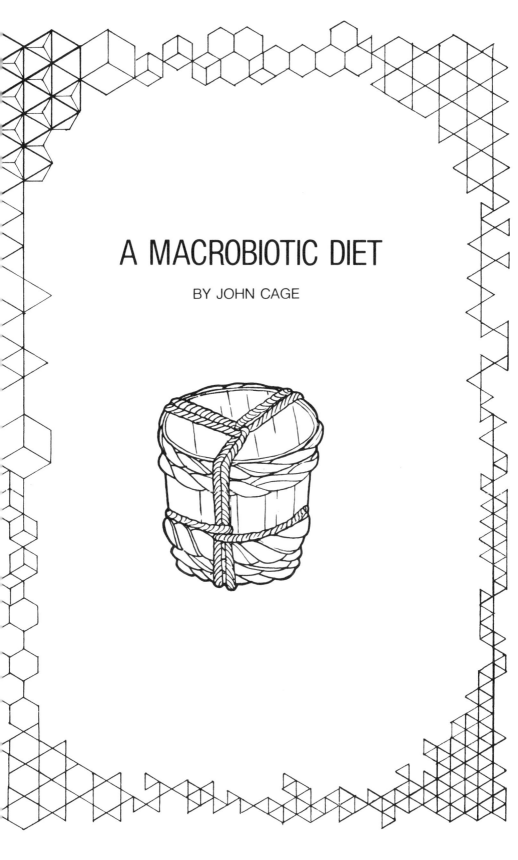

THE MACROBIOTIC DIET

The macrobiotic diet has a great deal to do
with yin and yang and finding a balance between them. I have not studied this carefully. All I try to observe is whether something suits me or not. Michio Kushi told me
I should eat more root vegetables and less
leafy ones, though he recommended watercress
and parsley. The basis of the diet is the
combination of brown rice and beans. This
makes a protein and the rice is very balanced.
I've become very fond of it. Nuts and seeds
are good; and vegetables may be eaten. They
are good when their sugars are slightly car-
amelized (slightly burned). This is a mat-
ter of taste rather than diet. Some vegetables
should be avoided: potatoes, tomatoes, egg-
plant and peppers. Turnips, carrots, celeriac,
the large white Japanese radishes (daikon); all
these are good. When possible eat not only the
root but the leaves too of these (including
a little of the carrot leaves). In this direction (away from beans and rice, towards
the right or sugar), avoid sugar. Eat as
little fruit as you fail to resist. Or become very choosy; insist on the best wild
strawberries, raspberries, and melons. Honey
is sugar. Don't use it. Wine, and I suppose
beer, vodka, and whiskey are also sugar.
These (particularly single malt) I still can't
resist. Liquids should be reduced during the
day (including water, tea, etc.) to two quarts.
In the other direction towards meat, you can
eat a little chicken or fish, avoid shell fish
and eat eggs not too often, although they are
permitted. Avoid red meat and all dairy pro-
ducts. The idea is to make a shift from the
animal fats to the vegetable oils, and to reduce the liquids. Instead of brown rice you
can have cous-cous, kasha, bulgur (cracked
wheat). As far as quantities go, you should

eat mostly rice, then beans, then vegetables, and least chicken or fish. Salads are not good because they are too liquid. One very good way to prepare dandelion or endive (the American green curly endive or chicory) is to chop it up and saute it in a little oil; then add tamari (health food soy sauce).

TABOULI

2 cups fine cracked wheat
1 cup ice cold water
2 cups minced fresh parsley
1 cup finely chopped scallions
3 Tbs. minced fresh mint
3/4 cup lemon juice
1 cup olive oil (health food store variety)
1 tsp. salt
½ tsp. black pepper (or more. Black pepper is ok.)

Combine wheat and water and refrigerate for 1 hour. Add remaining ingredients. Refrigerate. Garnish with whatever (radishes, olives, avocado).

BROWN RICE

Twice as much water as rice. If you wish, substitute a very little wild rice for some of the brown. Wash. Add a small amount of hijiki (seaweed). Bring to a good boil. Cover with cloth and heavy lid and cook for 20 minutes over medium flame; reduce flame to very low and cook 30 minutes more. Uncover. If it is not sticking, cook it some more. If it is sticking to the bottom of the pan, stir it a little and then cover again and let it rest with the fire off. When you look at it again, it will have loosened itself from the bottom of the pan.

SESAME RICE

For 4 cups hot cooked brown rice, saute 2
tablespoons of cashews or more in 4 tablespoons of oil (sesame) and 1 cup sesame seeds.
Continue until seeds are golden. Add 1 teaspoon sea salt. Mix with rice.

FRIED RICE

Saute scallions. Add sliced celery, sesame
seeds if desired, and mushrooms, with tamari
at the end. A fair amount of tamari. Perhaps a little lemon juice.

WALNUT CHICKEN

Marinate chicken breasts cut into 1" cubes in
3 tablespooons tamari, 1 tablespoon sherry, $\frac{1}{2}$
teaspoon ground ginger or $\frac{1}{2}$" piece of fresh
ginger overnight. Heat 3 tablespoons sesame
oil (total = $\frac{1}{4}$ cup) over high flame and stir-
fry 3 sliced scallions, garlic clove cut in
two, and 1 cup coarsely chopped walnuts. After three or four minutes remove garlic and
transfer scallions and walnuts to a bowl. Add
remaining oil and chicken pieces and marinade.
Stir-fry about five minutes, until chicken is
tender and coated with soy mixture. Combine
with walnuts and scallions. Serve with rice.

ROAST CHICKEN

Get a good chicken not spoiled by agribusiness.
Place in Rohmertopf (clay baking dish with
cover) with giblets. Put a smashed clove of
garlic and a slice of fresh ginger between
legs and wings and breast. Squeeze the juice
of 2 or 3 fresh lemons over the bird. Then
an equal amount of tamari. Cover. Place in
cold oven turned up to 425°. Leave for 1
hour. Then uncover for 15 minutes, heat on,
to brown. Or use hot mustard and cumin seeds
instead of garlic. Keep lemon, tamari, garlic.

MISO SOUP

About 3 heaping tablespoons of miso paste.
There are as many kinds of this as there are
wines and cheeses. A few turnips, carrots,
and scallions. Any other vegetables. A
bunch of cress. In a little sesame oil,
saute the cut-up scallions, then the turnips
and carrots, not long. Then add 5 cups of
good water. When that comes to a boil, reduce the fire to low after removing a cup of
water to dissolve the miso paste in. Cover
and don't simmer longer than say 10 minutes.
Meanwhile you've soaked some Wakame (seaweed).
At the penultimate moment add the tenderest
vegetables (seaweed and cress); others you've
already put in. After turning out the flame,
add the cup of miso paste dissolved. Serve.

In hot weather, chill for about 20 minutes in
the freezer.

ZUCCHINI SPICED

Add salt, turmeric sparingly and finely chopped onion to heated oil. Stir for a minute,
add zucchini cut in pieces. Stir (covered)
for 5 minutes. Garnish with chopped nuts.

ZUCCHINI WITH SESAME BUTTER AND DILL

Cut each courgette lengthwise twice. Sear in
hot oil, cooking as quickly and as little as
possible. Then place in casserole with a
small amount of the oil and a sauce made of
tamari, fresh dill, and sesame butter or tahini. Place in moderate oven, for, say, 45
minutes.

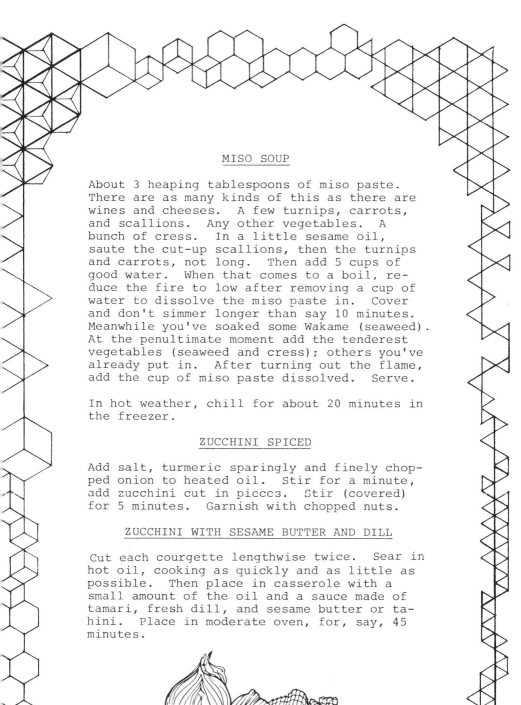

GRUEL BREAD

Go through refrigerator, collecting food that
you no longer wish to eat; rice, beans, cooked
vegetables or raw (parsley that's turned yellow, etc.). Include any liquids you may have
saved (such as water from parboiling string
beans). Put through Cuisinart and measure.
Add more than an equal amount of whole wheat
flour. Do not work with more than 5-7 cups
of gruel at a time. Mix and knead (adding
dry dill weed if wished) for about 45 minutes
or an hour, until it is consistent ("all of a
piece"). Then put in oiled bread pans. I
use corn oil. After putting it in, take it
out and put it back in upside down. (This
oils the entire loaf.) Take a wide knife and
make a deep indentation down the middle of the
loaf. Cover with damp cloth and leave in warm
place overnight. In the morning bake at 375°
for one hour and 15-20 minutes.

NUT BREAD

Follow the recipe above but use very few left-
overs (rice and string bean water are fine).
Add roasted unsalted nuts (walnuts, filberts,
Brazil nuts, almonds, cashews, etc.). The
nuts should be cut, but not very finely.

These breads are good with peanut butter (make
you own in a Cuisinart). Or smoked salmon (the
Gruel Bread only). Or a slice of avocado. Or
alone.

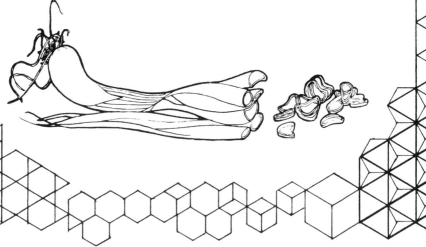

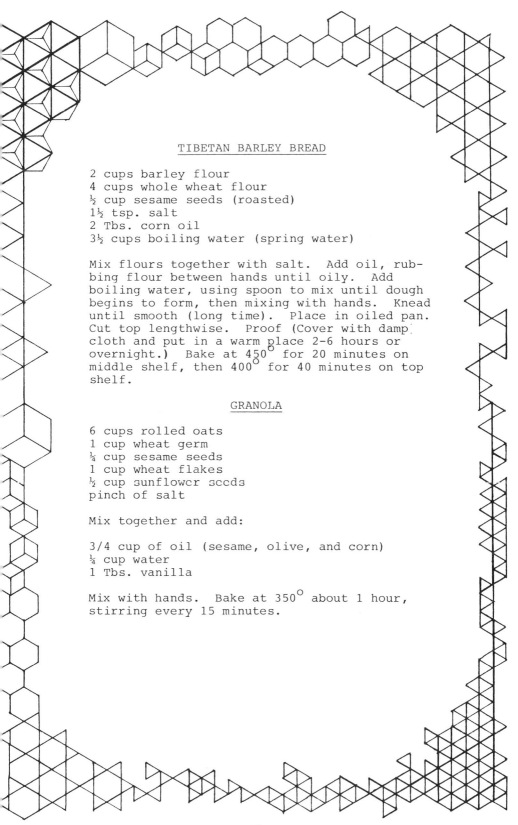

TIBETAN BARLEY BREAD

2 cups barley flour
4 cups whole wheat flour
½ cup sesame seeds (roasted)
1½ tsp. salt
2 Tbs. corn oil
3½ cups boiling water (spring water)

Mix flours together with salt. Add oil, rubbing flour between hands until oily. Add boiling water, using spoon to mix until dough begins to form, then mixing with hands. Knead until smooth (long time). Place in oiled pan. Cut top lengthwise. Proof (Cover with damp cloth and put in a warm place 2-6 hours or overnight.) Bake at 450° for 20 minutes on middle shelf, then 400° for 40 minutes on top shelf.

GRANOLA

6 cups rolled oats
1 cup wheat germ
¼ cup sesame seeds
1 cup wheat flakes
½ cup sunflower seeds
pinch of salt

Mix together and add:

3/4 cup of oil (sesame, olive, and corn)
¼ cup water
1 Tbs. vanilla

Mix with hands. Bake at 350° about 1 hour, stirring every 15 minutes.

BEANS

Soak beans overnight after having washed them.
In the morning change the water and add Kombu
(seaweed). Also, if you wish, add rosemary
or cumin. Watch them so that they don't cook
too long, just until tender. Then pour off
most of the liquid, saving it, and replace
it with tamari. Taste to see whether it's
too salty. If it is, add more bean liquid.
Then if you have the juice from a roasted
chicken, put several tablespoons of this with
beans. If not, add some lemon juice. And the
next time you have roast chicken, add some of
the juice to the beans. Black turtle beans
or small white beans can be cooked without
soaking overnight. But large kidney beans or
pinto beans, etc., are best soaked.

CHICK PEAS (GARBANZAS)

Soak several hours. Then boil in new water.
Until tender. They can then be used in many
ways:

1. Salad. Make a dressing of lemon or lime
with olive oil (a little more oil than lemon)
sea salt and black pepper, fresh dill, parsley,
and a generous amount of fine French mustard
(e.g. Pommery)
2. Or use with cous cous having cooked them
with ginger and a little saffron.
3. Or make homous. Place, say, 2 cups of
chick peas with ½ cup of their liquid in
Cuisinart. Add a teaspoon salt, lots of
black pepper, a little oil, and lemon juice
to taste.

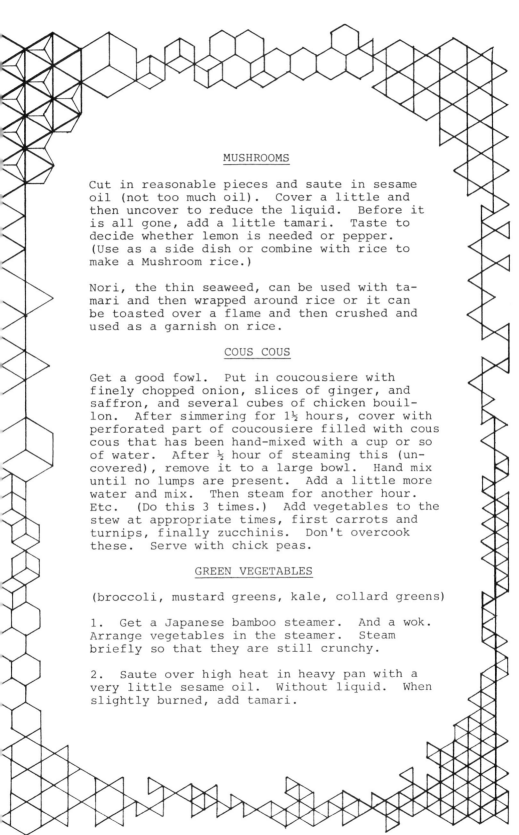

MUSHROOMS

Cut in reasonable pieces and saute in sesame
oil (not too much oil). Cover a little and
then uncover to reduce the liquid. Before it
is all gone, add a little tamari. Taste to
decide whether lemon is needed or pepper.
(Use as a side dish or combine with rice to
make a Mushroom rice.)

Nori, the thin seaweed, can be used with tamari and then wrapped around rice or it can
be toasted over a flame and then crushed and
used as a garnish on rice.

COUS COUS

Get a good fowl. Put in coucousiere with
finely chopped onion, slices of ginger, and
saffron, and several cubes of chicken bouil-
lon. After simmering for 1½ hours, cover with
perforated part of coucousiere filled with cous
cous that has been hand-mixed with a cup or so
of water. After ½ hour of steaming this (uncovered), remove it to a large bowl. Hand mix
until no lumps are present. Add a little more
water and mix. Then steam for another hour.
Etc. (Do this 3 times.) Add vegetables to the
stew at appropriate times, first carrots and
turnips, finally zucchinis. Don't overcook
these. Serve with chick peas.

GREEN VEGETABLES

(broccoli, mustard greens, kale, collard greens)

1. Get a Japanese bamboo steamer. And a wok.
Arrange vegetables in the steamer. Steam
briefly so that they are still crunchy.

2. Saute over high heat in heavy pan with a
very little sesame oil. Without liquid. When
slightly burned, add tamari.

STEAMED FISH FILLETS

Fish fillets are good steamed over slices of fresh ginger placed in a shallow dish to keep the juices and sprinkled with lemon juice and tamari.

SQUASH
(acorn, etc.)

Bake without cutting open at 425° for one hour and 15-30 minutes. (Do the same with any root vegetables.)

STRING BEANS

Parboil 7 minutes. Or if they are the fine small French ones, just 4 minutes. Make a dip of dampened wasabi (Japanese horseradish, with enough water to form a ball) with tamari.

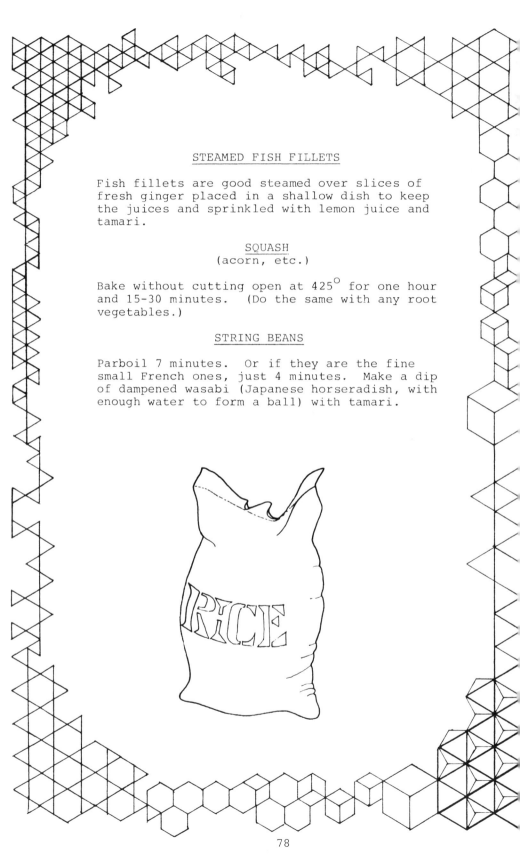

SALADS AND VEGETABLES

GREEN SALAD AND THREE VINEGAR DRESSING

Prepare at least two kinds of lettuce, bibb, endive, chicory, romaine, etc., but NOT iceberg. It must be two kinds.

For dressing mix in the bottom of the bowl:

2 Tbs. olive oil
1 Tbs. vinegar: equal amounts tarragon, cider, and wine
Season with mustard. Dip tines of fork into jar of mustard, what remains on tines, mix in dressing.

garlic, ½ clove chopped
1 canned pimento, chopped
1 tsp. capers

Mix well and toss with lettuce. Makes 2-3 servings.

CUCUMBER SALAD

3 cucumbers peeled, sliced very thin. Sprinkle generously with salt and let stand for ½ hour or longer until limp. Rinse cucumbers well with water, drain well...
Dressing for cucumber salad:
1 medium onion chopped fine
¼ cup of white vinegar
¼ cup crushed ice
generous sprinkling freshly ground pepper

Sprinkle crushed ice on cucumbers, chopped onion, add vinegar and pepper. Mix.

Margaret Mead

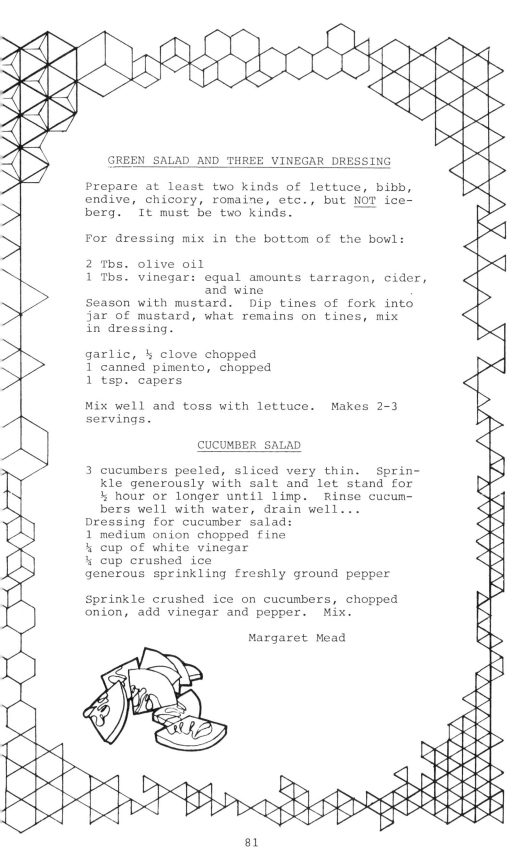

* * * * * * * * * * * *

**An Invitation to Seek the Future
In Celebration of the Present**

*If you would have the future,
take aim squarely at the present!*

*For it is precisely in the present
that the future is born.*

*You cannot predetermine the
form it will take.*

*But you can create a context
for its unfolding.*

*Make it a most propitious one!
The choice is yours to make.*

*Remember, too, each day, and
each and every hour of the day
that failing the present will diminish
or delay the future you desire.*

*Do not languish after something
which, in fact, is gone!*

*Think instead of building, now,
that which soon enough could be!*

*That which, in fact, has every
chance to be.*

*Extinguish anxiety!
Celebrate yourself in the present.*

*Decide that everything will
be alright.*

*Behave as if it were already so!
And, if it ever could have been,
it will be!*

*Keep your hopes alive.
Do not hang the present on them,
or the future either.*

*Just keep them alive because you
choose, in faith and courage to do so!*

*You may not know it but the world
is growing you.*

*So grow!
And grow and grow and grow.*

The way of courage is the only way!

©1981
Peter Keith Aborn

* * * * * * * * * * * *

<u>ODE TO THE WINGED BEAN</u>
(Psophocarpus Tetragonalobus)

No politicking hogwash
No vote-seeking hokus-pokus;
Real nitrogen enfixing
Genus psophocarpus
Tetragonalobus.

Soup and french-cut,
Formally served,
Not only did bloat us,
But also pleased our palates--
Long podded psophocarpus
Tetragonalobus.

Purple, yellow, brown and green;
Sometimes spotted
Sometimes clean.
Grotesquely knotted,
Roots unseen,
Why do they call you
Winged Bean?

Noduled tuber,
Pole bean tall,
Flower, seed, pod,
Edible all.
Who's the fairest
Bean of all?
Soy or psophocarpus
Tetraglonalobus?

Buckminster Fuller
Friday the 13th
January, 1978
Manila, Philippines

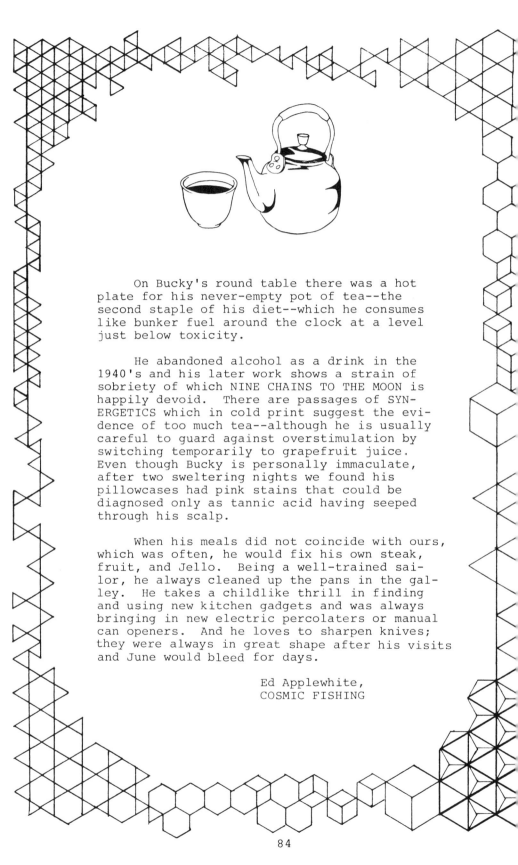

On Bucky's round table there was a hot
plate for his never-empty pot of tea--the
second staple of his diet--which he consumes
like bunker fuel around the clock at a level
just below toxicity.

He abandoned alcohol as a drink in the
1940's and his later work shows a strain of
sobriety of which NINE CHAINS TO THE MOON is
happily devoid. There are passages of SYN-
ERGETICS which in cold print suggest the evi-
dence of too much tea--although he is usually
careful to guard against overstimulation by
switching temporarily to grapefruit juice.
Even though Bucky is personally immaculate,
after two sweltering nights we found his
pillowcases had pink stains that could be
diagnosed only as tannic acid having seeped
through his scalp.

When his meals did not coincide with ours,
which was often, he would fix his own steak,
fruit, and Jello. Being a well-trained sai-
lor, he always cleaned up the pans in the galley. He takes a childlike thrill in finding
and using new kitchen gadgets and was always
bringing in new electric percolaters or manual
can openers. And he loves to sharpen knives;
they were always in great shape after his visits
and June would bleed for days.

> Ed Applewhite,
> COSMIC FISHING

On the day afer Pearl Harbor, I ran into
Bucky who was then working on <u>Fortune</u> outside
the old Time-Life Building in Rockefeller Center. As was our then custom, I suggested
that we go across the street and have a drink.
With no show of emotion or giving any sign of
inner determination, he said, "John, there's
a war on. And if I'm going to be of any use
to my country, I'm not going to take another
drink." And he never did. He went to work
for the War Production Board, and I never saw
him again until after the war was over.

John Fistere

TABBOULIEH

5 bunches of parsley
2 bunches of mint
6 young spring onions,
6 ripe tomatoes
½ cup good olive oil
juice of two lemons
1 cup of burghul (cracked wheat)

This is a salad we learned to love in our
years in Lebanon. Chop the parsley and the
mint fine--use your Cuisinart if you have
one, else your own slow scissors. Now cut
up the young onion, peel and chop tomatoes,
and combine all ingredients. Meantime you
have been soaking the burghul in boiling
water--drain off in a sieve, and squeeze dry.
Now pour on and mix the olive oil, and finally, the lemon juice. This is served in Lebanon on a great platter surrounded by the
young leaves of the heart of romaine and
these are used as little spades to spoon up
the salad and eat it.

Isobel Fistere

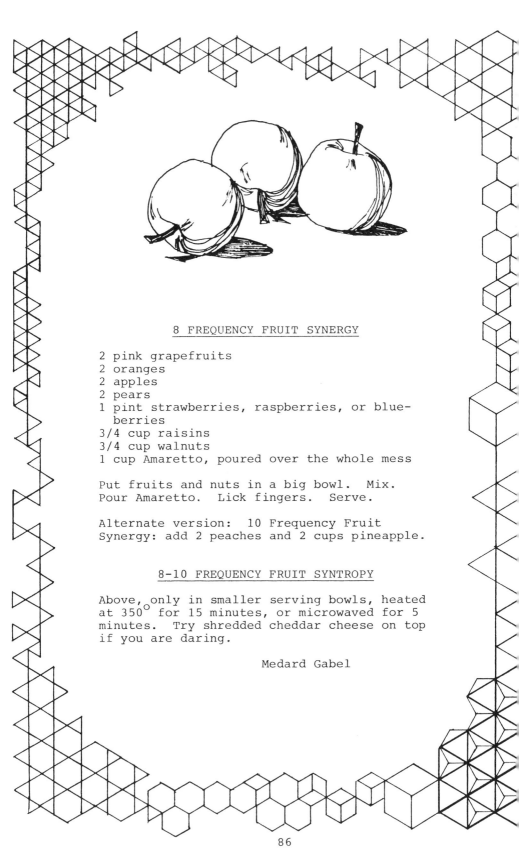

8 FREQUENCY FRUIT SYNERGY

2 pink grapefruits
2 oranges
2 apples
2 pears
1 pint strawberries, raspberries, or blueberries
3/4 cup raisins
3/4 cup walnuts
1 cup Amaretto, poured over the whole mess

Put fruits and nuts in a big bowl. Mix.
Pour Amaretto. Lick fingers. Serve.

Alternate version: 10 Frequency Fruit
Synergy: add 2 peaches and 2 cups pineapple.

8-10 FREQUENCY FRUIT SYNTROPY

Above, only in smaller serving bowls, heated
at 350° for 15 minutes, or microwaved for 5
minutes. Try shredded cheddar cheese on top
if you are daring.

Medard Gabel

GINGER-GARLIC SALAD DRESSING

Serves 8 to 10

1 fresh lemon
½ cup olive oil
1 tsp. fresh, grated ginger
1-2 cloves grated garlic (to taste)
2 leaves of fresh sweet basil
1 sprig of fresh winter savory
3 leaves of fresh tarragon
1 sprig of fresh dill*
salt and pepper to taste
4-5 drops of soy sauce

Chop fresh herbs. Squeeze lemon juice, combine with olive oil, salt, pepper, and soy
sauce. Fresh lettuce from the garden makes
a delicious salad.

*may use herbs of your choice

                    Ruth Asawa Lanier

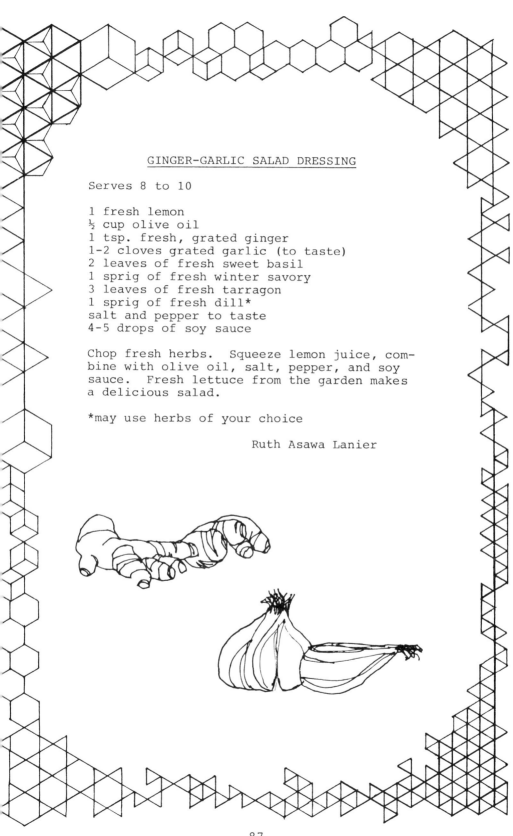

ONE CHAIN TO A ROOM

For R.B.F.

by Roger Hewlett July 12, 1938

("If even one-quarter of the inhabitants of
this earth stood on each other's shoulders
there'd be no need for chains on potty-chairs."
Confucius)

Oh, his name is Bucky Fuller
And he comes from Milton town
And they ran him out of college cause he
Wouldn't settle down
And he couldn't seem to do a thing
Like any normal man
So he went and joined the Navy
And he married Lady Anne.
And he sold a lot of building blocks
Like doughnuts, mostly hole
And he built a house of milk and steel
And hung it on a pole.

    (Now, I'm convinced you all must feel
     That it was rather droll
     To build a house of milk and steel
     And hang it on a pole.)

And when they laughed he shouted back
To tell them they were wrong
And he wrote a book to prove it
In words three meters long
Saying houses should be built on bolts
Like Mr. Ford's machines.
And people poked their neighbors, asking,
"You know what he means?"
"Like motor cars" he shouted.
"Here, I'll show you if you wish."
And he went and built a motor car
That acted like a fish.

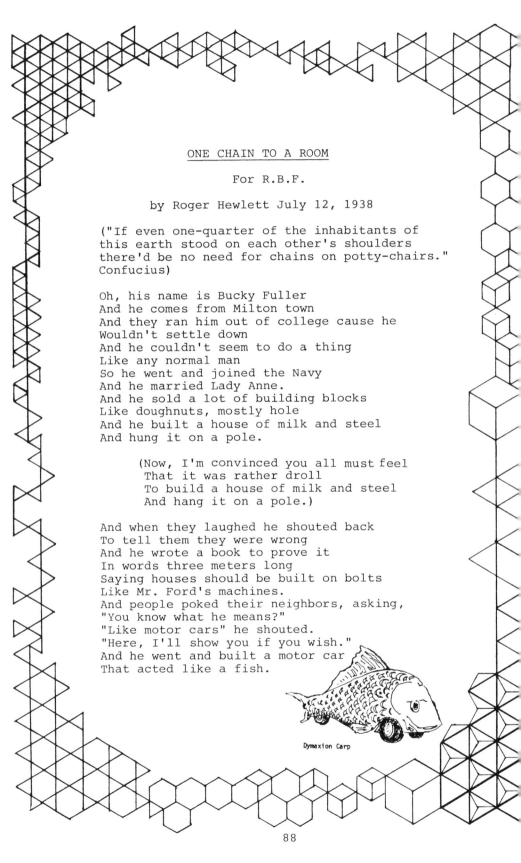

Dymaxion Carp

88

(To me, it's doubtful that a man
 Is ever going to wish
 To have his Twin Deluxe Sedan
 Behaving like a fish.)

Now, these few things that Bucky's done
I can't condone as such,
But then again, they're harmless
And they haven't hurt me much.
But he should have been contented
With his building and his car
Instead of forcing me to say
That he has gone too far.
For instead of leaving potties
Simple potties to remain
The fool has built a potty chair
That hasn't any chain.

(Now, call me stubborn if you dare
 But still I will maintain
 The world won't take a potty chair
 That hasn't any chain!)

For what is there to fiddle with
While sitting on the seat?
To rattle on the whited wall
In syncopated beat?
You may tell us what to drive, my boy,
And how to build our floors
But your words will never penetrate
Beyond the fast-closed doors.
You may dictate all you like, my boy,
But never will we hark
While we sit and swing our sil'vry chain
In coruscating arc.
And in the records of our hearts
Your name shall be a stain
As the man who built a potty chair
That hasn't any chain.

(And those that love him still despair
 That Bucky is the name
 Of the man who built the potty chair
 That hasn't any chain.)

SAUTÉED CUCUMBERS (JAPAN)

Sautéeing cucumbers brings out their delicate
flavor.

3 large cucumbers, peeled
2-3 Tbs. butter
salt and pepper
¼ cup chicken stock
2-3 Tbs. chopped dill or 2 tsp. dried dill
¼ lemon, juice only (optional)

Cut cucumbers into triangles (American cucumbers should be halved and seeded first).
Melt butter and sauté cucumbers briefly; they
should be almost cooked through, not raw, but
still crunchy. Add chicken stock and cook two
minutes longer or until liquid cooks off.
Sprinkle with dill and lemon juice and serve
immediately. Serves 4.

Steve Parker

ASPARAGUS DIPPING SAUCE

1 bunch asparagus
3 Tbs. light-colored miso (from oriental food
    store)
3 Tbs. sugar
2 Tbs. lemon juice

Steam asparagus until tender but not droopy.
Mix other ingredients thoroughly. Adjust
proportions to taste. Serve with asparagus
as dipping sauce, or serve together.

Kiyoshi Kuromiya

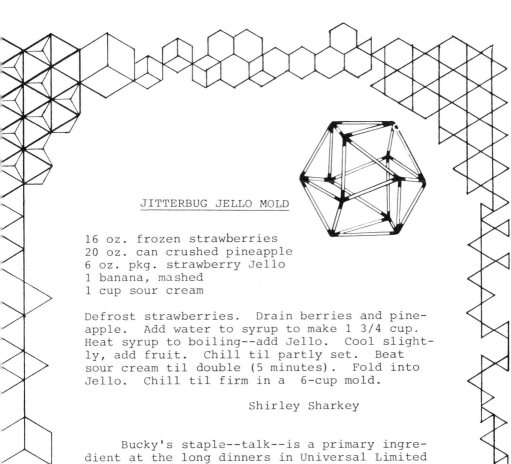

JITTERBUG JELLO MOLD

16 oz. frozen strawberries
20 oz. can crushed pineapple
6 oz. pkg. strawberry Jello
1 banana, mashed
1 cup sour cream

Defrost strawberries. Drain berries and pineapple. Add water to syrup to make 1 3/4 cup.
Heat syrup to boiling--add Jello. Cool slightly, add fruit. Chill til partly set. Beat
sour cream til double (5 minutes). Fold into
Jello. Chill til firm in a 6-cup mold.

                    Shirley Sharkey

     Bucky's staple--talk--is a primary ingre-
dient at the long dinners in Universal Limited
Art Edition's white kitchen or during lunches
outside under the catalpa tree. The artist
who is working that day sits in the place of
honor, at the head of the table. Friends,
printers, staff, and guests range around. The
food is an important part of Universal Limited's
ritual. Bucky declined everything except for
the tea, which he drinks incessantly and in a
quantity that easily qualifies him for the "en-
raptured fireplug" description his biographer
Hugh Kenner once employed in an article for the
New York Times. During his time at Universal
Limited, he managed to forgo all culinary plea-
sures except steak, spinach, and Jello. With
that menu, repeated three times a day, he had
reduced from a high of 206 pounds of too solid
flesh and with that menu he intended to maintain his accomplishment.

                    Amei Wallach, from the
                    introduction to
                    TETRASCROLL

Bil Baird's Marionettes

When Bucky was awarded a medal from the National Arts Club on Gramercy Park--Susie and I presented a shadow show--the life of RBF in lieu of a speech.

As I remember this piece is a collection of pundits trying to explain Bucky.

Bil and Susanna Baird

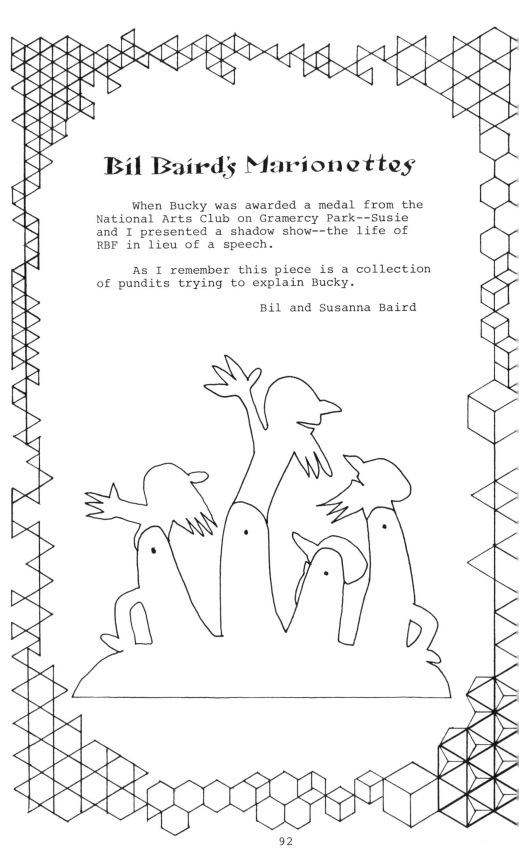

DESSERTS

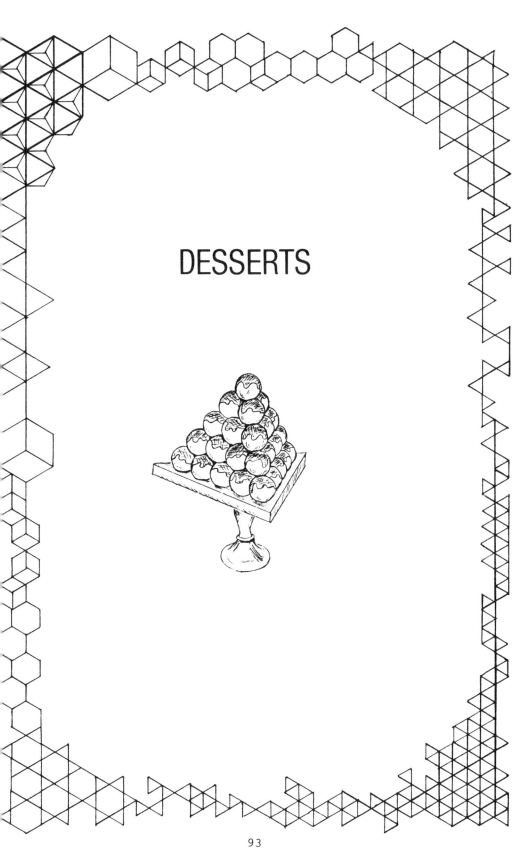

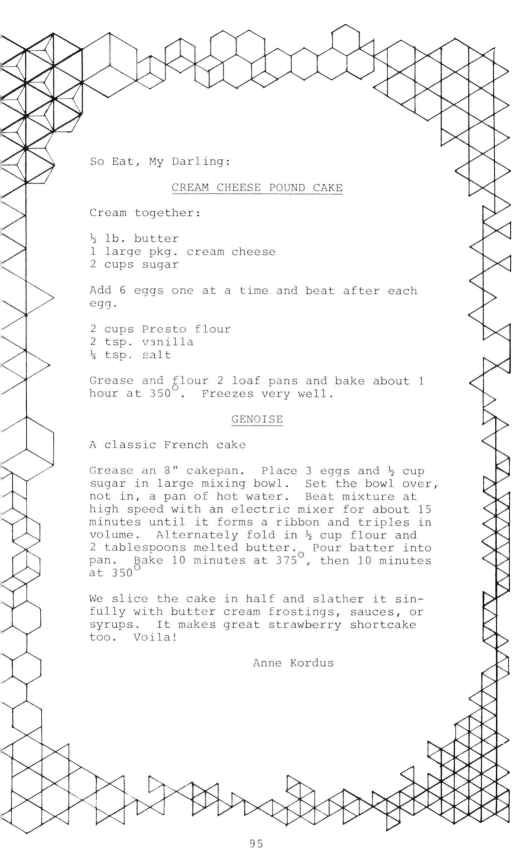

So Eat, My Darling:

CREAM CHEESE POUND CAKE

Cream together:

½ lb. butter
1 large pkg. cream cheese
2 cups sugar

Add 6 eggs one at a time and beat after each
egg.

2 cups Presto flour
2 tsp. vanilla
¼ tsp. salt

Grease and flour 2 loaf pans and bake about 1
hour at 350°. Freezes very well.

GENOISE

A classic French cake

Grease an 8" cakepan. Place 3 eggs and ½ cup
sugar in large mixing bowl. Set the bowl over,
not in, a pan of hot water. Beat mixture at
high speed with an electric mixer for about 15
minutes until it forms a ribbon and triples in
volume. Alternately fold in ½ cup flour and
2 tablespoons melted butter. Pour batter into
pan. Bake 10 minutes at 375°, then 10 minutes
at 350°

We slice the cake in half and slather it sin-
fully with butter cream frostings, sauces, or
syrups. It makes great strawberry shortcake
too. Voila!

Anne Kordus

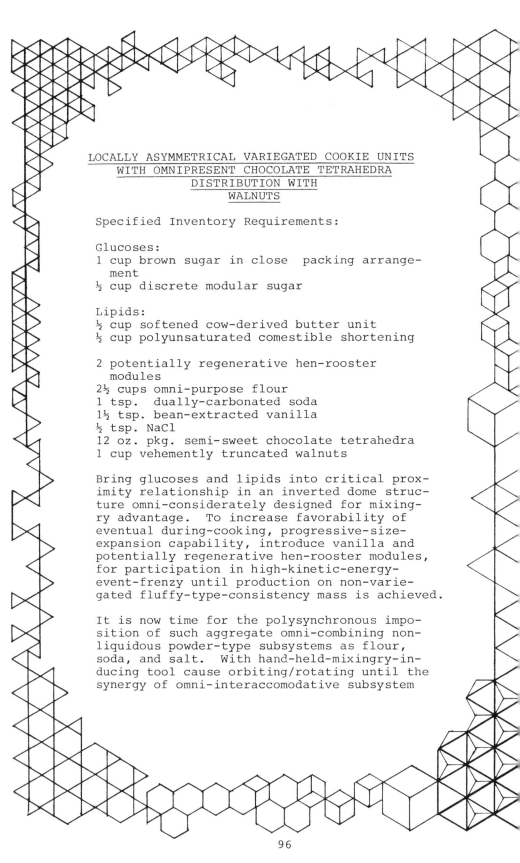

LOCALLY ASYMMETRICAL VARIEGATED COOKIE UNITS WITH OMNIPRESENT CHOCOLATE TETRAHEDRA DISTRIBUTION WITH WALNUTS

Specified Inventory Requirements:

Glucoses:
1 cup brown sugar in close packing arrangement
½ cup discrete modular sugar

Lipids:
½ cup softened cow-derived butter unit
½ cup polyunsaturated comestible shortening

2 potentially regenerative hen-rooster
modules
2½ cups omni-purpose flour
1 tsp. dually-carbonated soda
1½ tsp. bean-extracted vanilla
½ tsp. NaCl
12 oz. pkg. semi-sweet chocolate tetrahedra
1 cup vehemently truncated walnuts

Bring glucoses and lipids into critical prox-
imity relationship in an inverted dome structure omni-considerately designed for mixing-
ry advantage. To increase favorability of
eventual during-cooking, progressive-size-
expansion capability, introduce vanilla and
potentially regenerative hen-rooster modules,
for participation in high-kinetic-energy-
event-frenzy until production on non-varie-
gated fluffy-type-consistency mass is achieved.

It is now time for the polysynchronous impo-
sition of such aggregate omni-combining non-
liquidous powder-type subsystems as flour,
soda, and salt. With hand-held-mixingry-in-
ducing tool cause orbiting/rotating until the
synergy of omni-interaccomodative subsystem

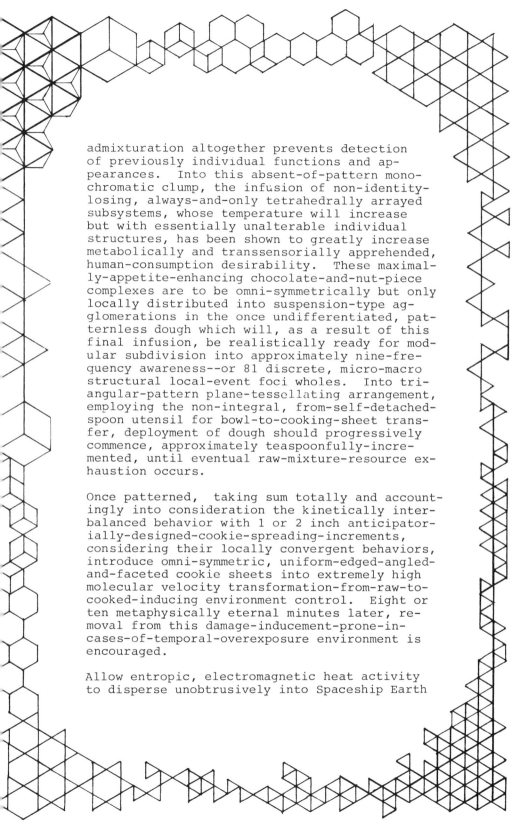

admixturation altogether prevents detection
of previously individual functions and ap-
pearances. Into this absent-of-pattern mono-
chromatic clump, the infusion of non-identity-
losing, always-and-only tetrahedrally arrayed
subsystems, whose temperature will increase
but with essentially unalterable individual
structures, has been shown to greatly increase
metabolically and transsensorially apprehended,
human-consumption desirability. These maximal-
ly-appetite-enhancing chocolate-and-nut-piece
complexes are to be omni-symmetrically but only
locally distributed into suspension-type ag-
glomerations in the once undifferentiated, pat-
ternless dough which will, as a result of this
final infusion, be realistically ready for modular subdivision into approximately nine-fre-
quency awareness--or 81 discrete, micro-macro
structural local-event foci wholes. Into tri-
angular-pattern plane-tessellating arrangement,
employing the non-integral, from-self-detached-
spoon utensil for bowl-to-cooking-sheet transfer, deployment of dough should progressively
commence, approximately teaspoonfully-incre-
mented, until eventual raw-mixture-resource ex-
haustion occurs.

Once patterned, taking sum totally and account-
ingly into consideration the kinetically inter-
balanced behavior with 1 or 2 inch anticipator-
ially-designed-cookie-spreading-increments,
considering their locally convergent behaviors,
introduce omni-symmetric, uniform-edged-angled-
and-faceted cookie sheets into extremely high
molecular velocity transformation-from-raw-to-
cooked-inducing environment control. Eight or
ten metaphysically eternal minutes later, re-
moval from this damage-inducement-prone-in-
cases-of-temporal-overexposure environment is
encouraged.

Allow entropic, electromagnetic heat activity
to disperse unobtrusively into Spaceship Earth

Galley until entire array of cookie complexes
are cool, and the high velocity, energetical-
ly-operative constellation of aroma-event-
stimuli's o'erwhelment of local sensory detection, integral-olfactory-tool functioning has
been broadcastingly accomplished. They are
now ready for maximum eatingry enjoyment, such
as never before experienced or even dreamt of
before the Design Science Cookie Revolution.

Synergetically produced
by the research kitchens
of the Buckminster Fuller
Institute

WACKY CAKE (DEVIL'S FOOD)
=========================

Put in ungreased square cake pan:

1½ cups sifted flour
1 cup granulated sugar
3 Tbs. cocoa
1 Tbs. baking soda
½ tsp. salt.

Stir until evenly mixed. Make 3 holes in
mix. In one, pour 5 tablespoons melted oleo;
in another, 1 tablespoon vinegar; in the other;
1 teaspoon vanilla. Pour 1 cup cold water over
all and mix until smooth. Bake at 350° for 35
minutes. Do not use as layer cake.

Connie Thelander

I was born in Milton town, seven miles
from the center of Boston. It was dominated
by the smell of chocolate from the Walter
Baker chocolate mills. The Walter Baker chocolate mills had a water wheel in its early
days and many buildings, some new but mostly
old, some going back to the Revolutionary War.
The smell of the chocolate was extremely
pleasant...

Buckminster Fuller

CHOCOLATE FROSTED BROWNIE CAKE

2 sq. unsweetened chocolate
½ cup butter
1 cup sugar
2 eggs
½ tsp. vanilla
¼ cup flour
¼ tsp. salt
1 cup chopped walnuts

Frosting:

3 Tbs. butter
2/3 cup chocolate chips

Preheat oven to 310°. Grease and flour 8"
cake pan. Melt chocolate and butter together
and stir in sugar. Add 2 eggs and vanilla and
beat like mad. Stir in flour and salt, then
walnuts. Bake for 40 minutes. Cool about 15
minutes, remove from pan and cool completely.
Coat with icing made by melting together butter and chocolate chips. Refrigerate til set.

Shirley Sharkey

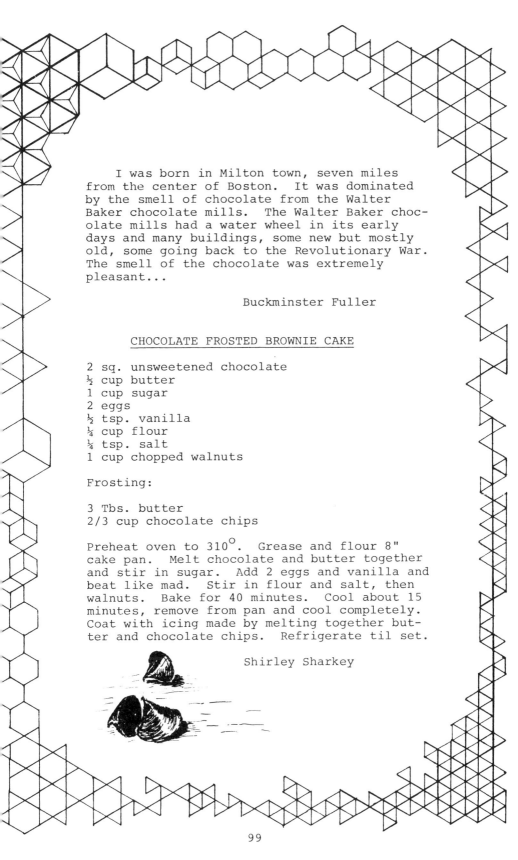

Here's a recipe, for batter or worse.

PUNAPPLE PIE

You have made it clear on several occasions, Bucky, that you are not especially fond of puns. Maybe it is because they were offered plain. Possibly you will change your mind after trying this punapple pie.

Because both puns and punapples come without a peel, their preparation is simple. It's the pie shell that takes the doing. A lot of crust is needed to present good friends with this pie and have confidence as you do it. You may even have to offer another fruit as well to accomplish this with a plum.

Punapples are packaged two ways: 12 to a box or 144. I much prefer the gross ones. Most of them are grown in Arizona where Superman's long time admirer, Miss Lane, has settled. Whenever you encounter these delicacies, it is quite likely they will have come from the Lois Farm of Yuma.

Also in the human interest vain is the fact that Mrs. Jemima, the pancake lady, asked about producing these pies. We wrote her saying, "In order to be really big in this business, you will need to be taller, Aunt."

If someone should give you a punapple pie, Bucky, you should first cut it into quarters, then divide each of these pieces in half. Next, sprinkle pickle preserves on top. When asked how you liked it, you can say you eight it with relish.

An ingredient urgently needed to be added to the recipe at this point is shortening...so I will.

Don Moore

PINEAPPLE PILOT FOR SPACESHIP EARTH

1 stick butter
2/3 cup sugar
1 lb. crushed pineapple with juice
1/8 tsp. salt
3 egg whites
½ cup sliced almonds
1½ cups crushed vanilla wafers
3 egg yolks

Mix butter, sugar, and egg yolks, and beat
until creamy. Add crushed pineapple and
sliced almonds to mixture; then beat egg
whites with salt, and fold into rest of ingredients. Top with crushed vanilla wafers
and chill for 12 hours before serving.

Pete Simoneaux

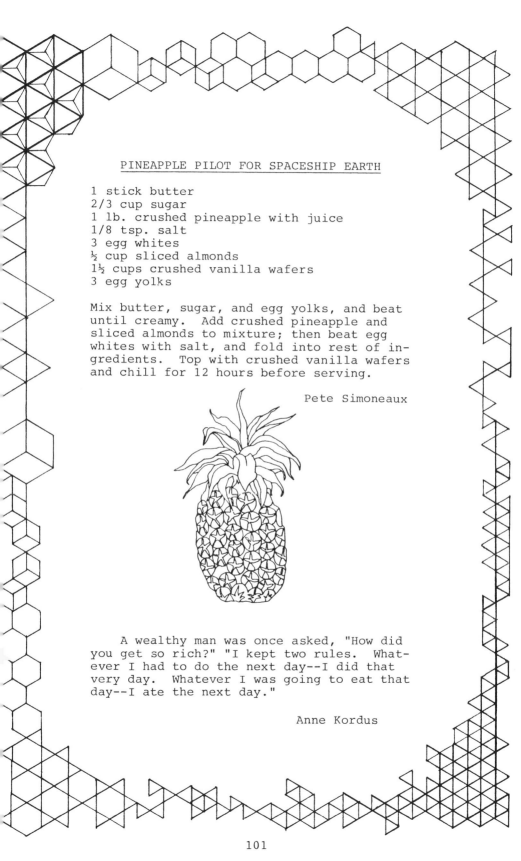

A wealthy man was once asked, "How did
you get so rich?" "I kept two rules. Whatever I had to do the next day--I did that
very day. Whatever I was going to eat that
day--I ate the next day."

Anne Kordus

CLUB INDIAN PUDDING

1 qt. scalded milk
5 tsp. corn meal
2 Tbs. butter
2 cup dark molasses
2 eggs, well beaten
½ tsp. cinnamon
1 tsp. salt
½ tsp. ginger (or nutmeg)
1 cup cold milk

Add corn meal to scalded milk gradually and cook and stir in a double boiler for 20 minutes. During the last 5 minutes, add butter, molasses, seasonings, and eggs. Turn into a buttered baking dish and pour the cold milk over the mixture. Bake at 325 to 350° (according to your oven) for about 1½ hours. Serve hot with ice cream.

Karl Menninger

GILDING THE LILY PART II

Skin but do not stone a peach. Brush lightly with a weak mixture of clear golden syrup (corn syrup) or melted brown sugar and brandy. Heat more brandy in a soupspoon. Ignite, and pour over the peach. Eat immediately.

A particular favorite of Bucky's.

Cedric Price

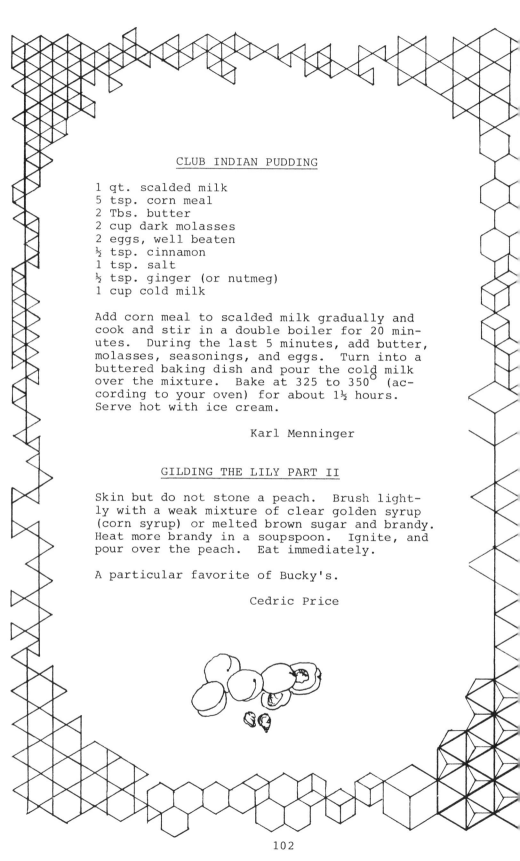

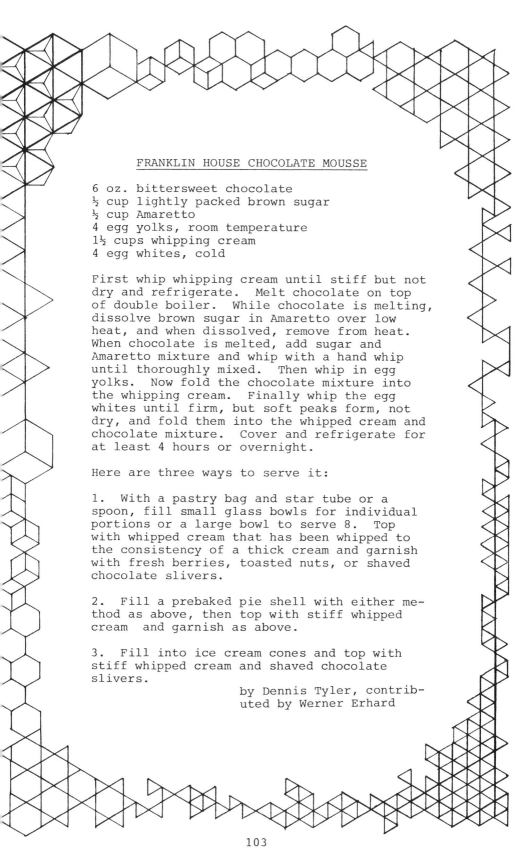

FRANKLIN HOUSE CHOCOLATE MOUSSE

6 oz. bittersweet chocolate
½ cup lightly packed brown sugar
½ cup Amaretto
4 egg yolks, room temperature
1½ cups whipping cream
4 egg whites, cold

First whip whipping cream until stiff but not
dry and refrigerate. Melt chocolate on top
of double boiler. While chocolate is melting,
dissolve brown sugar in Amaretto over low
heat, and when dissolved, remove from heat.
When chocolate is melted, add sugar and
Amaretto mixture and whip with a hand whip
until thoroughly mixed. Then whip in egg
yolks. Now fold the chocolate mixture into
the whipping cream. Finally whip the egg
whites until firm, but soft peaks form, not
dry, and fold them into the whipped cream and
chocolate mixture. Cover and refrigerate for
at least 4 hours or overnight.

Here are three ways to serve it:

1. With a pastry bag and star tube or a
spoon, fill small glass bowls for individual
portions or a large bowl to serve 8. Top
with whipped cream that has been whipped to
the consistency of a thick cream and garnish
with fresh berries, toasted nuts, or shaved
chocolate slivers.

2. Fill a prebaked pie shell with either method as above, then top with stiff whipped
cream and garnish as above.

3. Fill into ice cream cones and top with
stiff whipped cream and shaved chocolate
slivers.

                    by Dennis Tyler, contrib-
                    uted by Werner Erhard

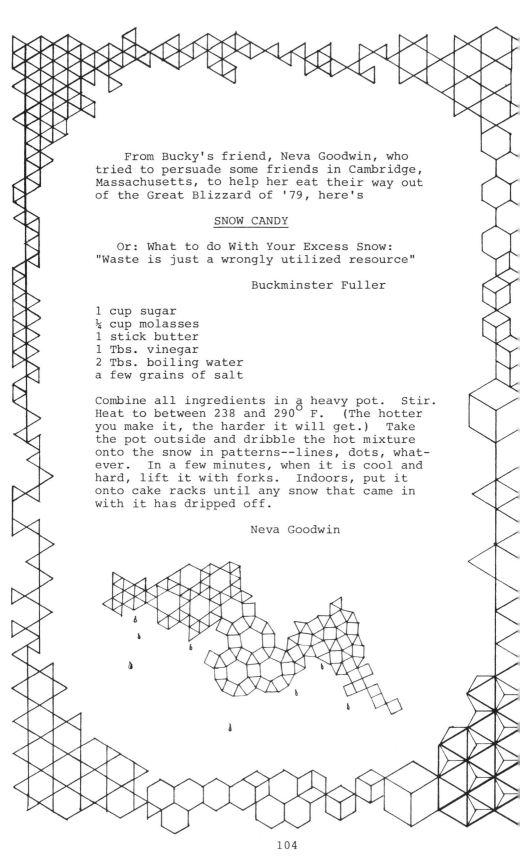

From Bucky's friend, Neva Goodwin, who tried to persuade some friends in Cambridge, Massachusetts, to help her eat their way out of the Great Blizzard of '79, here's

SNOW CANDY

Or: What to do With Your Excess Snow:
"Waste is just a wrongly utilized resource"

Buckminster Fuller

1 cup sugar
¼ cup molasses
1 stick butter
1 Tbs. vinegar
2 Tbs. boiling water
a few grains of salt

Combine all ingredients in a heavy pot. Stir. Heat to between 238 and 290° F. (The hotter you make it, the harder it will get.) Take the pot outside and dribble the hot mixture onto the snow in patterns--lines, dots, whatever. In a few minutes, when it is cool and hard, lift it with forks. Indoors, put it onto cake racks until any snow that came in with it has dripped off.

Neva Goodwin

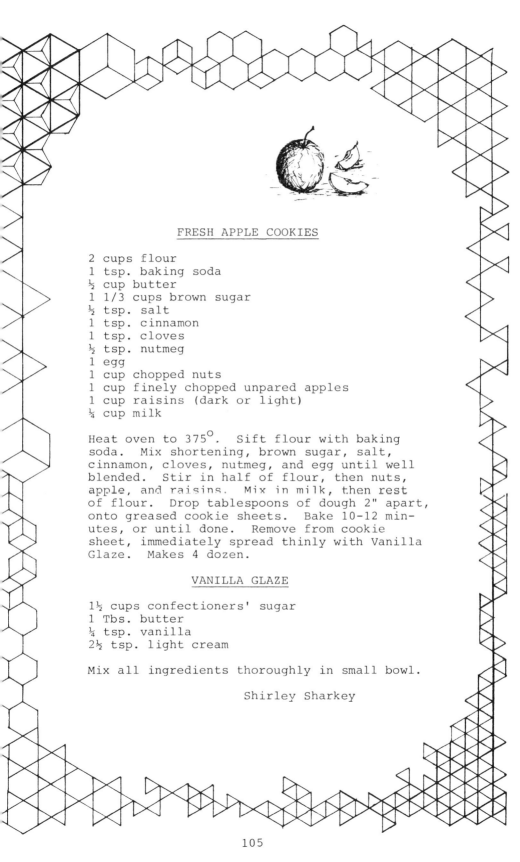

FRESH APPLE COOKIES

2 cups flour
1 tsp. baking soda
½ cup butter
1 1/3 cups brown sugar
½ tsp. salt
1 tsp. cinnamon
1 tsp. cloves
½ tsp. nutmeg
1 egg
1 cup chopped nuts
1 cup finely chopped unpared apples
1 cup raisins (dark or light)
¼ cup milk

Heat oven to 375°. Sift flour with baking
soda. Mix shortening, brown sugar, salt,
cinnamon, cloves, nutmeg, and egg until well
blended. Stir in half of flour, then nuts,
apple, and raisins. Mix in milk, then rest
of flour. Drop tablespoons of dough 2" apart,
onto greased cookie sheets. Bake 10-12 minutes, or until done. Remove from cookie
sheet, immediately spread thinly with Vanilla
Glaze. Makes 4 dozen.

VANILLA GLAZE

1½ cups confectioners' sugar
1 Tbs. butter
¼ tsp. vanilla
2½ tsp. light cream

Mix all ingredients thoroughly in small bowl.

                    Shirley Sharkey

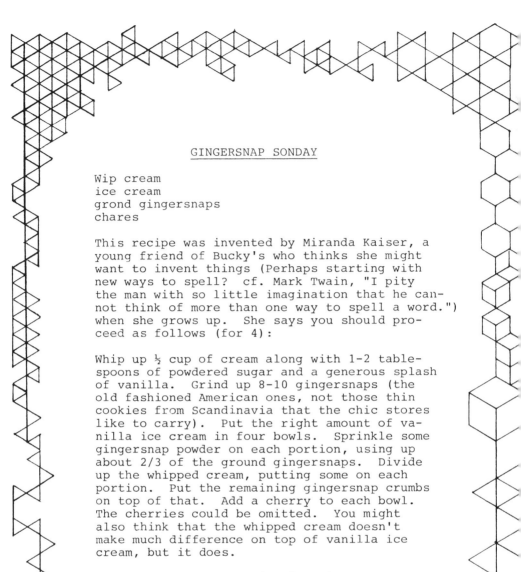

GINGERSNAP SONDAY

Wip cream
ice cream
grond gingersnaps
chares

This recipe was invented by Miranda Kaiser, a
young friend of Bucky's who thinks she might
want to invent things (Perhaps starting with
new ways to spell? cf. Mark Twain, "I pity
the man with so little imagination that he cannot think of more than one way to spell a word.")
when she grows up. She says you should pro-
ceed as follows (for 4):

Whip up ½ cup of cream along with 1-2 tablespoons of powdered sugar and a generous splash
of vanilla. Grind up 8-10 gingersnaps (the
old fashioned American ones, not those thin
cookies from Scandinavia that the chic stores
like to carry). Put the right amount of vanilla ice cream in four bowls. Sprinkle some
gingersnap powder on each portion, using up
about 2/3 of the ground gingersnaps. Divide
up the whipped cream, putting some on each
portion. Put the remaining gingersnap crumbs
on top of that. Add a cherry to each bowl.
The cherries could be omitted. You might
also think that the whipped cream doesn't
make much difference on top of vanilla ice
cream, but it does.

Miranda Kaiser

FOGGUN FRAPPE

2 cups orange juice
2 scoops of favorite ice cream
1 dash of Amaretto or Kahlua

Put in blender. Blend. Drink. Repeat.

Medard Gabel

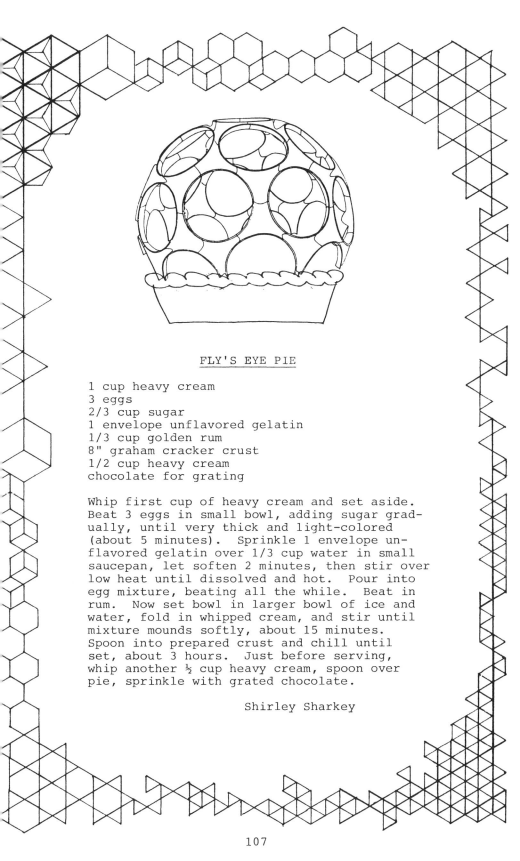

FLY'S EYE PIE

1 cup heavy cream
3 eggs
2/3 cup sugar
1 envelope unflavored gelatin
1/3 cup golden rum
8" graham cracker crust
1/2 cup heavy cream
chocolate for grating

Whip first cup of heavy cream and set aside.
Beat 3 eggs in small bowl, adding sugar gradually, until very thick and light-colored
(about 5 minutes). Sprinkle 1 envelope unflavored gelatin over 1/3 cup water in small
saucepan, let soften 2 minutes, then stir over
low heat until dissolved and hot. Pour into
egg mixture, beating all the while. Beat in
rum. Now set bowl in larger bowl of ice and
water, fold in whipped cream, and stir until
mixture mounds softly, about 15 minutes.
Spoon into prepared crust and chill until
set, about 3 hours. Just before serving,
whip another ½ cup heavy cream, spoon over
pie, sprinkle with grated chocolate.

Shirley Sharkey

FULLER BLEND

In 1977, when we were preparing to open
our first exhibition with Bucky, I asked Ed
Schlossberg if there were any preparations we
should make for the vernissage. Ed advised
us to be prepared to serve Bucky a large
amount of tea during his visit. It was a simple request. At a staff meeting, we decided
that in order to be good hosts, we should
have an assortment of tea from all over the
world. We were fortunate to have Bucky with
us for several days and were surprised at the
quantity of tea that he consumed. Near the
end of the last day, we ran out of tea and
panic spread everywhere. Someone ran to the
local grocery and replenished our supply.
Bucky was finishing an interview when I gave
him a fresh cup. He took a sip, leaned back
in his chair, and sighed, "Ah, Lipton." I
ran to the kitchen, and of course, we had
finally hit the spot. It was Lipton.

Ronald Feldman

METRICALLY BABY

Won't you be my metrically baby
Couple on a low-cal date
Less of you and less of me is dandy
Provided we are only losing weight.

Pounds will vanish from our waistlines baby
Youthful clothes will once more fit
So let's lose every bit
For instance, where we sit
Or else we may be
Melonbelly too.

(to be sung to the tune of Melancholy Baby)

Buckminster Fuller

108

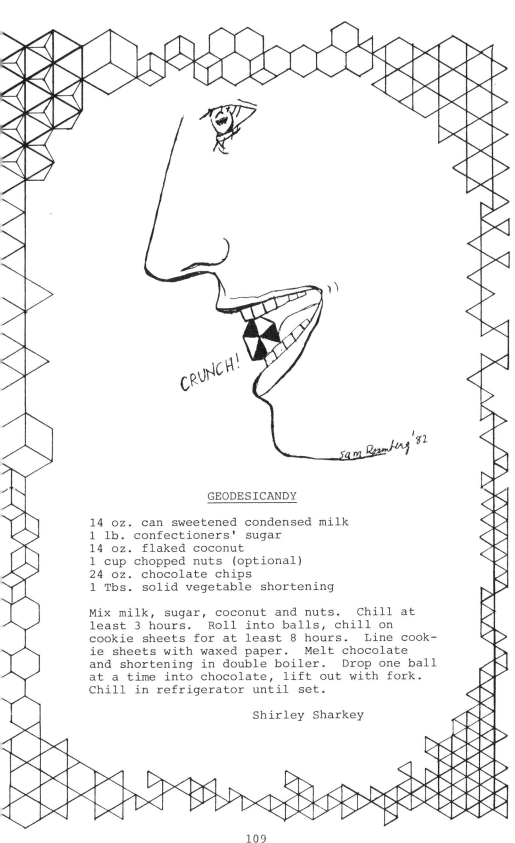

CRUNCH!

sam Rozenberg '82

GEODESICANDY

14 oz. can sweetened condensed milk
1 lb. confectioners' sugar
14 oz. flaked coconut
1 cup chopped nuts (optional)
24 oz. chocolate chips
1 Tbs. solid vegetable shortening

Mix milk, sugar, coconut and nuts. Chill at
least 3 hours. Roll into balls, chill on
cookie sheets for at least 8 hours. Line cookie sheets with waxed paper. Melt chocolate
and shortening in double boiler. Drop one ball
at a time into chocolate, lift out with fork.
Chill in refrigerator until set.

Shirley Sharkey

SIMPLE TREATS FOR BUCKY'S EATS

These are little specialties to add a feeling of home to wherever Bucky may be on his orbitings around the Earth.

Ever since his hip operation he has stuck to his hardy recovery breakfast...a true

COMPREHENSIVE CEREAL

For 1 bowl:

Prepare 2 serving size of any old fashioned oatmeal (no salt). When it is just about ready add a handful of raisins or cut prunes; stir in and let the pot finish cooking; then let it sit for a few minutes. In the cereal bowl, add a handful of Kellogg's "Cracklin Bran" and Post "Grapenuts." Stir oatmeal in with dry cereal and a little non-fat milk. Serve with non-fat milk, and your best silver spoon.

RICHARD'S RHUBARB

Another simple dessert treat which Bucky has loved ever since he was a little boy is rhubarb. It is a dessert he loves, particularly when he's trimming down.

Take one package of frozen or fresh cut rhubarb and put in a Pyrex dish. Cover and heat in oven at 350° until it is tender (so it breaks with a fork). Stir in honey to taste. Stir enough so that it is all broken up, an even smooth consistency.

PENOBSCOT PARSNIPS

Bucky has also always loved parsnips but finds people seldom cook them these days. Once when we were together living and working

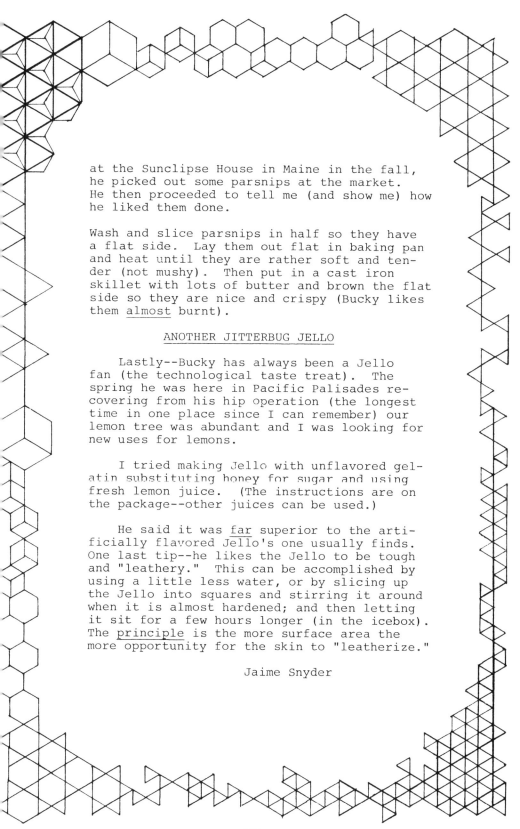

at the Sunclipse House in Maine in the fall,
he picked out some parsnips at the market.
He then proceeded to tell me (and show me) how
he liked them done.

Wash and slice parsnips in half so they have
a flat side. Lay them out flat in baking pan
and heat until they are rather soft and tender (not mushy). Then put in a cast iron
skillet with lots of butter and brown the flat
side so they are nice and crispy (Bucky likes
them almost burnt).

ANOTHER JITTERBUG JELLO

Lastly--Bucky has always been a Jello
fan (the technological taste treat). The
spring he was here in Pacific Palisades re-
covering from his hip operation (the longest
time in one place since I can remember) our
lemon tree was abundant and I was looking for
new uses for lemons.

I tried making Jello with unflavored gelatin substituting honey for sugar and using
fresh lemon juice. (The instructions are on
the package--other juices can be used.)

He said it was far superior to the arti-
ficially flavored Jello's one usually finds.
One last tip--he likes the Jello to be tough
and "leathery." This can be accomplished by
using a little less water, or by slicing up
the Jello into squares and stirring it around
when it is almost hardened; and then letting
it sit for a few hours longer (in the icebox).
The principle is the more surface area the
more opportunity for the skin to "leatherize."

Jaime Snyder

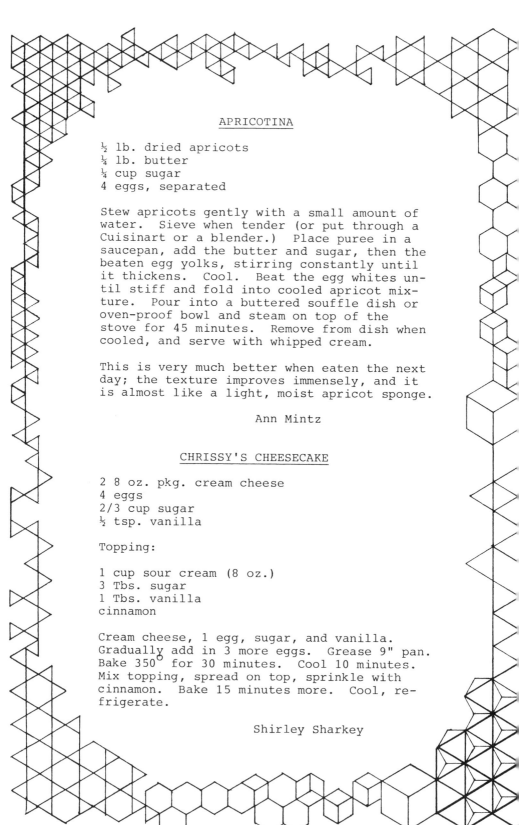

APRICOTINA

½ lb. dried apricots
¼ lb. butter
¼ cup sugar
4 eggs, separated

Stew apricots gently with a small amount of
water. Sieve when tender (or put through a
Cuisinart or a blender.) Place puree in a
saucepan, add the butter and sugar, then the
beaten egg yolks, stirring constantly until
it thickens. Cool. Beat the egg whites until stiff and fold into cooled apricot mixture. Pour into a buttered souffle dish or
oven-proof bowl and steam on top of the
stove for 45 minutes. Remove from dish when
cooled, and serve with whipped cream.

This is very much better when eaten the next
day; the texture improves immensely, and it
is almost like a light, moist apricot sponge.

Ann Mintz

CHRISSY'S CHEESECAKE

2 8 oz. pkg. cream cheese
4 eggs
2/3 cup sugar
½ tsp. vanilla

Topping:

1 cup sour cream (8 oz.)
3 Tbs. sugar
1 Tbs. vanilla
cinnamon

Cream cheese, 1 egg, sugar, and vanilla.
Gradually add in 3 more eggs. Grease 9" pan.
Bake 350° for 30 minutes. Cool 10 minutes.
Mix topping, spread on top, sprinkle with
cinnamon. Bake 15 minutes more. Cool, re-
frigerate.

Shirley Sharkey

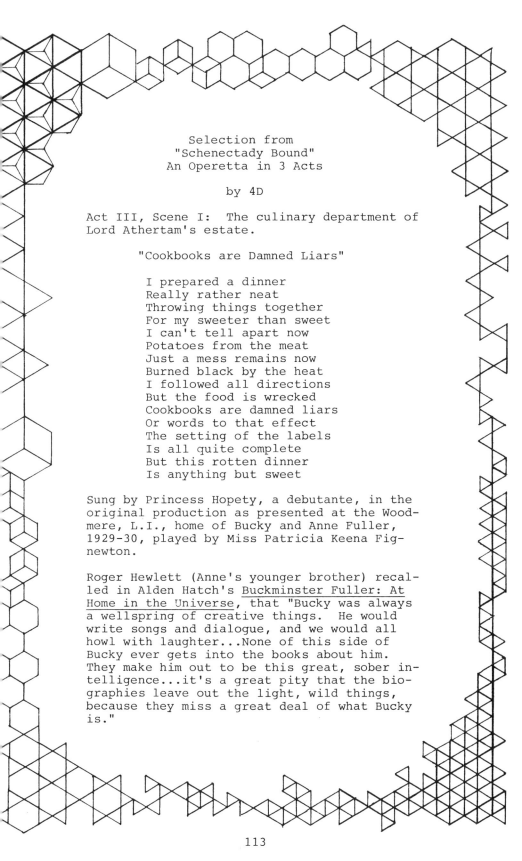

Selection from
"Schenectady Bound"
An Operetta in 3 Acts

by 4D

Act III, Scene I: The culinary department of
Lord Athertam's estate.

"Cookbooks are Damned Liars"

I prepared a dinner
Really rather neat
Throwing things together
For my sweeter than sweet
I can't tell apart now
Potatoes from the meat
Just a mess remains now
Burned black by the heat
I followed all directions
But the food is wrecked
Cookbooks are damned liars
Or words to that effect
The setting of the labels
Is all quite complete
But this rotten dinner
Is anything but sweet

Sung by Princess Hopety, a debutante, in the
original production as presented at the Wood-
mere, L.I., home of Bucky and Anne Fuller,
1929-30, played by Miss Patricia Keena Fig-
newton.

Roger Hewlett (Anne's younger brother) recal-
led in Alden Hatch's Buckminster Fuller: At
Home in the Universe, that "Bucky was always
a wellspring of creative things. He would
write songs and dialogue, and we would all
howl with laughter...None of this side of
Bucky ever gets into the books about him.
They make him out to be this great, sober intelligence...it's a great pity that the biographies leave out the light, wild things,
because they miss a great deal of what Bucky
is."

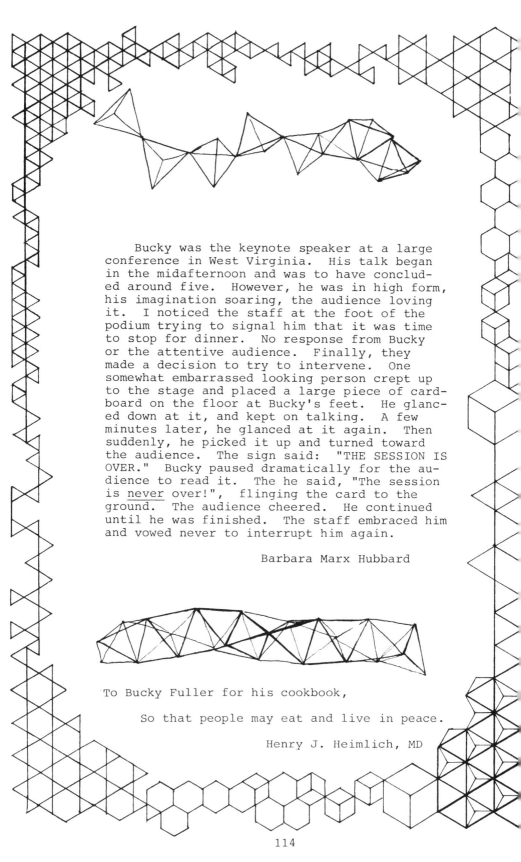

Bucky was the keynote speaker at a large conference in West Virginia. His talk began in the midafternoon and was to have concluded around five. However, he was in high form, his imagination soaring, the audience loving it. I noticed the staff at the foot of the podium trying to signal him that it was time to stop for dinner. No response from Bucky or the attentive audience. Finally, they made a decision to try to intervene. One somewhat embarrassed looking person crept up to the stage and placed a large piece of cardboard on the floor at Bucky's feet. He glanced down at it, and kept on talking. A few minutes later, he glanced at it again. Then suddenly, he picked it up and turned toward the audience. The sign said: "THE SESSION IS OVER." Bucky paused dramatically for the audience to read it. The he said, "The session is _never_ over!", flinging the card to the ground. The audience cheered. He continued until he was finished. The staff embraced him and vowed never to interrupt him again.

Barbara Marx Hubbard

To Bucky Fuller for his cookbook,

So that people may eat and live in peace.

Henry J. Heimlich, MD

INDEX

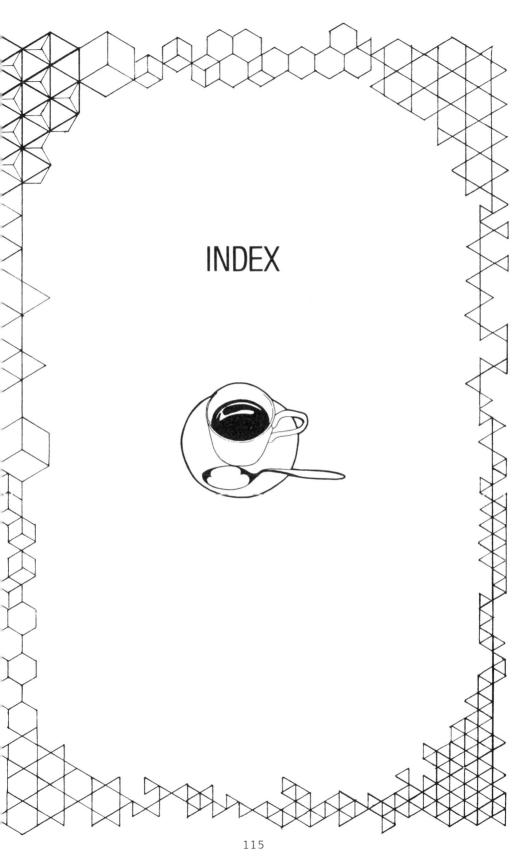

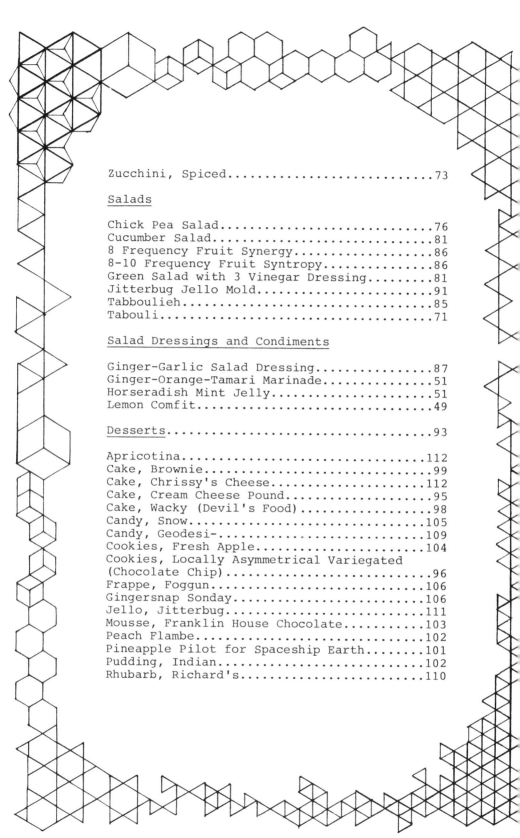

SYNERGETIC STEW   The Buckminster Fuller Institute
                    3501 Market Street
                    Philadelphia, PA   19104

☐ Send me _____ copies of SYNERGETIC STEW, at
  $7.95 per copy, postpaid.

☐ Send me further information on publications and maps,
  artifacts and gift items available from the Institute.

  Enclosed is my check or money order for $_____.

  Name_____

  Street_____

  City_____ State_____ Zip_____

SYNERGETIC STEW   The Buckminster Fuller Institute
                    3501 Market Street
                    Philadelphia, PA   19104

☐ Send me _____ copies of SYNERGETIC STEW, at
  $7.95 per copy, postpaid.

☐ Send me further information on publications and maps,
  artifacts and gift items available from the Institute.

  Enclosed is my check or money order for $_____.

  Name_____

  Street_____

  City_____ State_____ Zip_____

SYNERGETIC STEW   The Buckminster Fuller Institute
                    3501 Market Street
                    Philadelphia, PA   19104

☐ Send me _____ copies of SYNERGETIC STEW, at
  $7.95 a copy, postpaid.

☐ Send me further information on publications and maps,
  artifacts and gift items available from the Institute.

  Enclosed is my check or money order for $_____.

  Name_____

  Street_____

  City_____ State_____ Zip_____

Experiments in Food and Festivity

Jaime Snyder

I am excited to have the opportunity to introduce you to this new edition of *Synergetic Stew–Explorations in Dymaxion Dining.* The 1981 publication was a surprise gift for my grandfather, Buckminster Fuller, from his Philadelphia office staff on the occasion of his eighty-sixth birthday. It comprises stories and recipes gathered from many of his dear friends and family. As I reviewed a copy of the first edition, I was immediately reminded what a delightful publication it is, and especially how it reflects Bucky's great sense of humor, largely overlooked in the canon of articles and books about him.

Many people know that Bucky wrote "Roam Home to a Dome," a parody of "Home on the Range." But few are aware he also wrote a "musical extravaganza" in 1947–*Ezradoon,* based on the hit Lerner and Loewe Broadway show *Brigadoon*–which he performed for a special family celebration with his wife, Anne, and her nine siblings and their spouses. In *Synergetic Stew* there's also an excerpt from Bucky's "Schenectady Bound: An Operetta in 3 Acts," featuring his song "Cookbooks are Damned Liars" (see page 113). His daughter and my mother, Allegra Fuller Snyder, once told D. W. Jacobs, writer/director of the one-man show *R. Buckminster Fuller: THE HISTORY (and Mystery) OF THE UNIVERSE,* "You know, I think in his heart he longed to be a song-and-dance man."

As Bucky's brother-in-law Roger Hewlett reflected elegantly (see page 113): "Bucky was always a wellspring of creative things. He would write songs and dialogue, and we would all howl with laughter.... None of this side of Bucky ever gets into the books about him. They make him out to be this great, sober intelligence.... It's a great pity that the biographies leave out the light, wild things, because they miss a great deal of what Bucky is."

―――――

On Bucky's extensive schedule of lectures around the globe, he and Anne would often visit us in Los Angeles. During the holidays they would rent a furnished apartment near Allegra's for an extended stay: Anne enjoyed the warm Southern California weather, and Bucky was happy to take advantage of the time to work on his writing projects. Regardless of his world travels, Bucky always made a point of getting there early enough to go to the farmer's market in central L.A. to get the turkey and plenty of other fixin's for the celebration, and in time for Christmas Eve's tree trimming.

Bucky was all in for the holidays. I would watch closely as he prepared his special gravy, which would emerge out of the fat and drippings of the turkey– not to forget the well-cooked scrapings from the pan. He would carefully show aspiring culinary artists who might migrate through the kitchen exactly how he did it. It was "all about the roux," alchemically arising out of the pan from which the turkey had been removed to a proper platter. Fat, scrapings, flour, all cooked and thickened … mmm-mmm.

But it was the legendary eggnog which always stole the show. One Christmas he posted his recipe on the kitchen wall, revealing the secrets of his special brew. Later in my teens I came to enjoy the taste and buzz of it–but not the

Christmas Egg-nog

you. Many of you may think of Bucky as a "teetotaler". He was, however, up to the age of 47, quite a "heavy drinker." Then, on my mother and father's 25th wedding anniversary, he gave up both drinking or smoking and never did either again, after that day. His self-discipline was extraordinary . But my father was also a traditionalist. He loved traditional rituals and celebration. The gesture of a "toast" was a part of that traditional pattern.

Even when my father was traveling extensively he always made sure that he got home to be with all of us for Christmas. On Christmas Eve while the rest of us were trimming the Christmas tree my father would mix up this eggnog recipe. It was very much the tradition of our family that the tree was brought in after the children had gone to sleep, and all the tree trimming was done in the late hours of Christmas Eve, so that on the morning of Christmas Day, the children would wake up to an extraordinary vision of beauty and mystery. We would toast the Christmas in with a taste of the newly brewing eggnog A big family dinner on the following Christmas day was a central part of the Christmas celebrations, and the eggnog would usher in that celebration. My father loved all of these times of being together and towards the end of the Christmas day, he would usually begin to sing some songs or even launch into one of his wonderful clog dances. The spirit of the holidays and the eggnog gently dwindled away. The tree remained up till the 6th of Jan-uary -- "twelfth night" and with its dismantlement the last drop of the eggnog was consumed. It was this sense of tradition which created a very important balance or foundation for Bucky's sense of vision. We share the recipe with you as our "toast" to our shared vision for the future

10 Qts. Eggnog Milk
2 Qts. Bourbon Whiskey
1 Qt. Brandy
1 5th Sherry (1/2=13 oz)
3 Shakes Rum
Put Eggnog Milk in Big Cold Bowl
Mix All the Liquor Togeter and Pour in Slowly While Always Stirring the Eggnog Milk

Buckminster Fuller

Editor's note: Allegra Fuller Snyder, President of The Buckminster Fuller Institute had a few words to say about Bucky's Eggnog Recipe:

This rich and very alco-holic Christmas eggnog recipe, written by Bucky's own hand, may be a surprise to some of

rock-solid hangover for my untrained lightweight constitution. He once told me that in his early days of Christmas parties he would literally fill a bathtub with eggnog before adding all the other ingredients—lots of bourbon, rum, sherry, and brandy!

I imagine it was parties like these in the 1930s which carried on the tradition of the "Three Hours for Lunch Club," of which Bucky had been a member. He had been invited by his friend, mentor, and writer Christopher Morley, who inspired him to take his writing seriously—and put him together with J. B. Lippincott, who published his *Nine Chains to the Moon* in 1938. I'm quite confident the Club members were not needing extra lunch hours for sipping tea! However, in 1942, on the occasion of the Bucky and Anne's twenty-fifth wedding anniversary, he gave her the gift of "giving up drinking." And he never took it up again.

————

Bucky was quite stocky when I was growing up in the early 1960s. His weight eventually got up to 207 lbs. He described it as "carrying around two 35-pound suitcases" with him all the time. One of my early memories was when Bucky took up drinking one of the first liquid weight-loss foods: Metrecal. I can imagine the drink had both the appeal of being very efficient in terms of weight loss, as well as being convenient to use.

And then the cans were no more to be seen. Silently, without any fanfare, the experiment ended without any weight lost. However, there was one notable outcome: his delightful parody of the 1912 popular song "Melancholy Baby," which became "Metrically Baby" (see page 108).

Bucky was an extremely disciplined fellow. He even included a whole chapter in his book *Critical Path* entitled "Self Disciplines." One particular discipline comes to mind: "I never show people what I am working on until I have actually tackled the problem." Maybe this was at play when one day I greeted Bucky after a hiatus and all of a sudden, there he stood looking like a completely different person. He had lost a lot of weight and I had no idea how he had done it.

Somehow, out of nowhere, he had taken up a diet of steak and vegetables three times a day: no starches, no breads, no desserts—except Jell-O. And he drank copious amounts of black tea. In addition to the weight loss, he appreciated, as always, the convenience and efficiency of the new design. His office could just send a message ahead to each lecture venue with his prescribed menu. Thus, there wouldn't be any need to make countless dietary decisions tying up unnecessary energy. I've never heard a word about what exactly prompted this food regime. Ed Applewhite recounted that when queried, Bucky explained "the cows are eating much more vegetation and converting it to protein than [I] could possibly cope with firsthand" (see page 46).

He completely jettisoned those two 35-pound suitcases of unnecessary weight! As he would later say, "Who was that? It wasn't me." Returned to the weight of 137 pounds, and back to "fighting trim," he launched into a whole new era, well timed with the acceleration of his lectures and projects around the world.

————

In the late 1960s the month of August meant that all sorts of cousins, aunts, uncles, grandparents, and grandchildren would converge on Bear Island, off the coast of Maine. It was also a time when Bucky would host many of his friends and associates who might chance to visit. A day's adventures could include sailboat rides, visiting neighboring islands, or dunking in the bay's cold water, as well as projects like putting up a tensegrity dome on the southwest point. Certainly cooking was a big part of the fun, with lobsters available from the island's caretaker-fisherman, Pearl Hardie, as well as clams and mussels gathered from the beaches at low tide. When Isamu Noguchi visited one summer he turned everyone on to the culinary delicacy of raw sea urchins, and precisely how to prepare them—a big shift for our small minds, which only knew urchins were important to avoid stepping on! I recall him wet from gathering them in the bay, and then carefully carving out an opening in their geodesic dome shells to reveal the prized meat. On another occasion John Cage introduced islanders to the gold mine of native chanterelle mushrooms filling the woods, of which we had been unaware. We all picked them, and then he prepared them for the evening meal.

After the day's adventures, the family would gather in the Eating House for dinner. The dining room had two large white tables, one for the children and one for the adults, each seating a cozy dozen. Bucky would sit at the head of the table closest to the stone fireplace. Inevitably, after dinner, conversation would develop, which would usually induce him to respond to questions about some facet of life on our planet. The conversation would extend late into the evening. After all the family had eventually migrated back to the Big House, Bucky would often stay behind to work in the dining room, with a big pot of black tea and whatever manuscript was front and center in his attention.

Bucky edits a manuscript after dinner under a kerosene lamp at the dining room table of the Eating House at Bear Island (Photo by Jaime Snyder)

One morning we trickled into the Eating House for breakfast. There on the mantle of the stone fireplace sat carefully crafted signage in Bucky's familiar printing:

$$\text{The Law of Irreversibility}$$
$$1 \text{ gallon } T = 1 \text{ gallon } P$$
$$\text{but}$$
$$1 \text{ gallon } P \neq 1 \text{ gallon } T$$

We all drank a toast of tea to scientific precision!

————

In 1980 Bucky and Anne decided to rent a house right around corner from Allegra's on the west side of Los Angeles. Still Bucky kept his office in Philadelphia, while orbiting in and out of there and L.A. I had been living and writing music in Maine, but with the move I came and lived in my own wing of their new place, while I entered UCLA to study music composition.

During those last few years, Bucky dealt with a few health issues, the most significant of which was a hip replacement operation. The requirements of his recovery began to soften the boundaries of his strict steak diet. Oatmeal with prunes and milk became the morning staple, while Jell-O gave way to ice cream with an "occasional" cookie. Many of his favorite recipes, such as his well-done baked parsnips with lots of butter and brown sugar, found their was back into his diet. Together with a slight slowing in his pace, he gained a little weight (see pages 110 &111).

One day after he was back up and around, he and Anne invited his surgeon and wife, of whom they were very fond, over for a thank-you meal at the house. Bucky assured me he had it covered; he would set up the whole thing since I was busy at school. When I stopped by later in the afternoon I saw the dining room table set elegantly; and in the kitchen was a bucket of Kentucky Fried Chicken, and many little buckets of all the KFC side dishes: coleslaw, corn on the cob, mashed potatoes, gravy, and lots of rolls. I resisted the temptation to add my two cents.

One of the great joys of my life was sharing my musical journey with Bucky. During the period when I lived at my grandparents' summer home in Maine, on Deer Isle, Bucky visited often. He worked on his manuscripts while I worked on my first six songs. Then we'd compare notes. He was very encouraging of me, thrilled to see me discover my own voice, and became my first fan.

My last year at UCLA the Opera Workshop culminated with a production of Puccini's *Madame Butterfly.* I got a very small part in it, with one brief moment on stage as The Imperial Commissioner. My grandfather was not going to miss the performance, and made sure his schedule allowed for him to be in town. We were both feeling exhilarated as we returned home after the show, when Bucky stopped me at the front door. He turned to me and said: "You know, Jaime, I am really feeling that I might like to start some voice lessons. I feel that I really have the potential be a good singer!" Then he croaked out a few notes to demonstrate. Allegra was right: in his heart he longed to be a song-and-dance man.

For several years we had a potluck lunch for the entire staff about once a month–a great time to share ideas. (This venture has brought back so many great memories. I remembered that Meddy [Medard Gabel] was famous for his fruit salads; Kiyoshi [Kuromiya], for his sticky rice; Janice, hummus; and me, dessert.) At one of those lunches someone brought in one of the recipe-collection books sold by a church group in order to share a recipe. Then someone else jokingly said that we should do one of our own. At that time we were trying to come up with a unique gift for Bucky's birthday so the idea just grew from that. Synergy!

Shirley Sharkey
Former Executive Administrator of Fuller's office

R. Buckminster Fuller (1895–1983) was an architect, engineer, geometrician, cartographer, philosopher, futurist, inventor of the famous geodesic dome, and one of the most brilliant thinkers of his time. Fuller was renowned for his comprehensive perspective on the world's problems. For more than five decades, he developed pioneering solutions reflecting his commitment to the potential of innovative design to create technology that does "more with less" and thereby improve human lives. The author of nearly thirty books, he spent much of his life traveling the world lecturing and discussing his ideas with thousands of audiences. In 1983, shortly before his death, he received the U.S. Presidential Medal of Freedom, the nation's highest civilian honor, with a citation acknowledging that his "contributions as a geometrician, educator, and architect-designer are benchmarks of accomplishment in their fields." After Fuller's death, when chemists discovered a new carbon molecule with a structure similar to that of a geodesic dome, they named the molecule "buckminsterfullerene"–now commonly referred to in the scientific community as the *buckyball*.

Contributors

Peter Keith Aborn p. 82
Vice president of ISI (Institute for Scientific Information).

Ed Applewhite pp. 46, 84
Collaborator with Fuller on *Synergetics: Explorations in the Geometry of Thinking* (both volumes), Applewhite was known as a writer and as a former CIA officer. He is the author of *Cosmic Fishing: An Account of Writing* Synergetics *with Buckminster Fuller, Washington Itself: An Informal Guide,* and *Paradise Mislaid: Life, Death and the Human Predicament of Being Biological.*

Ruth Asawa Lanier pp. 28, 87
An American sculptor known for her iconic woven wire structures and for her activism in education and the arts, Asawa Lanier was a student of Fuller's at Black Mountain College, and they became fast friends thereafter. She founded the Alvarado Arts Workshop in 1968 for schoolchildren.

Bil Baird p. 92
An American puppeteer, Baird was known for creating Charlemagne the Lion; he also wrote *The Art of the Puppet* (1965). In a career that spanned more than sixty years, Baird and his puppets performed for millions. They toured Russia, India, Tibet, Afghanistan, and Turkey, and appeared in "The Lonely Goatherd" sequence in the film *The Sound of Music* (1965); Baird also provided the puppets for *Dark Shadows,* a television vampire soap opera in the 1960s.

Susanna Baird p. 92
Wife of puppeteer Bill Baird.

Peter Brown pp. 36, 37
Unknown.

John Cage pp. 70–78
An American composer, music theorist, artist, and philosopher, Cage was a pioneer of indeterminacy in music, electroacoustic music, and nonstandard use of musical instruments.

Lim Chong Keat p. 59
An architect and urban designer, Chong Keat cofounded Malayan Architects Co-Partnership and Architects Team 3, having a formative role in advancing architectural education and professionalization, and in the shaping of Singapore's urban development. Chong Keat coorganized "Campuan" intellectual exchanges in Bali and Penang with Buckminster Fuller (later revived as "Buckyworld Confluence").

Elizabeth Choy pp. 38, 55
Former staffer at Fuller's office.

John Ciardi p. 44
An American poet, translator, and etymologist, Ciardi published *How Does Poetry Mean?,* on how to read, write, and teach poetry.

John Denver p. 34
An American singer-songwriter, record producer, actor, activist, and humanitarian, Denver was one of the most popular acoustic artists of the 1970s.

Amy Edmondson pp. 16, 38, 65, 66, 68
The Novartis Professor of Leadership and Management at Harvard Business School, Edmondson's research examines leadership, learning, and innovation in teams and organizations, and has been published in numerous academic and managerial articles. She also worked for Buckminster Fuller and wrote *A Fuller Explanation: The Synergetic Geometry of R. Buckminster Fuller.*

Ted Ehmann p. 15
Salesman for the printing company Buckminster Fuller and his staff used to print their maps.

Werner Erhard pp. 17, 103
An American author, professor, and founder of the Erhard Seminars Training, Erhard was introduced to Fuller by Jaime Snyder. Erhard invited Bucky to give an all-day lecture at Town Hall in New York in 1976 produced by the Est Foundation, which led to a series of all-day programs entitled "Conversations with Buckminster Fuller" all over the country.

Ronald Feldman p. 108
Pioneering contemporary art dealer and founder of the Ronald Feldman Gallery in New York.

John and Isobel Fistere p. 85
Authors of *Jordan, the Holy Land* and *Jerusalem: A Guide to the Holy City. The Hashemite Kingdom of Jordan.*

Medard Gabel pp. 30, 31, 86, 106
Author, speaker, and one of original team working with Fuller on the World Game project; Gabel cofounded the World Game Institute, and later founded Big Picture Small World, Inc. Gabel is the author of *Earth, Energy, and Everyone* (1980) and *Hoping: Food for Everyone* (1979). With Global Education Motivators, he created the Design Science Lab, a workshop for developing strategies to address the UN Millennium Development Goals.

Eugene Garfield p. 67
Eugene Eli Garfield was an American linguist and businessman, one of the founders of bibliometrics and scientometrics. He founded the Institute for Scientific Information (ISI) in 1960. He helped to create *Current Contents, Science Citation Index, Journal Citation Reports,* and *Index Chemicus,* among others, and founded the magazine *The Scientist.*

Neva Goodwin p. 104
Neva Goodwin Rockefeller is codirector of the Global Development and Environment Institute (GDAE) at Tufts University, where she is

a research associate at the Fletcher School of Law and Diplomacy and director of the Social Science Library. She served as a board member of the Design Science Institute, founded in 1972 to support Fuller's initiatives.

d'Arcy Hayman   p. 8
Hayman was the International Arts Program director for UNESCO for twenty years (1960–1980). She was also a teacher, painter, and writer.

Henry J. Heimlich   p. 114
An American thoracic surgeon and medical researcher, Heimlich is widely credited as the inventor of what is now known as the Heimlich maneuver, a technique of abdominal thrusts for stopping choking.

Roger S. Hewlett   pp. 88, 89
Anne's youngest brother; a writer and editor at *Time* magazine and later a senior editor at *Sports Illustrated.*

Barbara Marx Hubbard   p. 114
Author, speaker, and cofounder/president of the Foundation for Conscious Evolution, Hubbard was the author of seven books on social and planetary evolution. In conjunction with the Shift Network, she coproduced the worldwide "Birth 2012" multimedia event.

Miranda Kaiser   p. 106
Copresident of the Refugee Center Online, a nonprofit that helps refugees and displaced persons successfully integrate in the United States and Italy, Kaiser is a member of the Council on Foreign Relations and serves as a trustee of the Rockefeller Family Fund and the David Rockefeller Fund.

Peter Kent   p. 6
Longtime member of Fuller's staff, and a great-nephew of Anne Fuller.

Anne Kordus   pp. 95, 101
Teddy Kordus raised and bred Rhododendrons. He and his wife, Anne, attended many of Bucky's talks, and he named one of his varietals after Anne Fuller.

Kiyoshi Kuromiya   pp. 29, 41, 90
A Japanese American author and pioneering civil rights and LGBTQ activist, Kuromiya worked closely with Fuller as adjuvant on his books *Critical Path, GRUNCH of Giants,* and *Cosmography* and as a longtime member of his staff.

Mae Lee   p. 47
Unknown.

Arthur Loeb   p. 33
A scientist, crystallographer, and a leader in field of design science, Loeb successfully combined the worlds of science and art, devising a language of spatial patterns that he described as "visual mathematics." A founder of the

International Society for the Interdisciplinary Study of Symmetry (ISIS-Symmetry), Loeb collaborated with such innovators as R. Buckminster Fuller and M. C. Escher.

Paula Martin   p. 21
Martin was an artists' model in New York in the 1920s and '30s and was a waitress at Romany Marie's.

Margaret Mead   pp. 46, 81
An American cultural anthropologist featured frequently as an author and speaker in the mass media during the 1960s and 1970s, Mead served as president of the American Association for the Advancement of Science in 1975. She is the author of *Coming of Age in Samoa* (1928) and *Sex and Temperament in Three Primitive Societies* (1935).

Karl Menninger   p. 102
An American psychiatrist and a member of the Menninger family of psychiatrists, who founded the Menninger Foundation and the Menninger Clinic in Topeka, Kansas.

Yehudi Menuhin   p. 45
An American-born violinist and conductor who spent most of his performing career in Britain, Menuhin is widely considered one of the greatest violinists of the twentieth century.

Margy Meyerson   pp. 11, 28, 32, 35, 57, 60, 112
Considered an expert in the field of urban planning, Meyerson was a joint editor of *Urban Housing* (1966), a landmark text still on syllabi at Berkeley and other city planning programs. A former member of the Philadelphia City Planning Commission, she is active with many civic groups, including the Rosenbach Museum & Library, where she is Chair Emeritus.

Martin Meyerson   p. 11
A United States city planner and academic leader best known as the president of the University of Pennsylvania between 1970 and 1981, Meyerson, through his research, mentorship, essays, and consulting, exerted formative influence on US postwar urban policy at the municipal and federal levels.

Ann Mintz   pp. 28, 32, 35, 58, 60, 112
The author of memoirs, essays, and travel writing and also a musician, Mintz served on Bucky's staff as an archivist.

Don Moore   p. 100
An engineer-designer, Moore worked at RCA Whirlpool and in 1957 patented a robot floor cleaner. He worked with Fuller on the development of numerous projects and crewed on Fuller's sailboats in the 1960s.

Ed Muskie   p. 18
An American statesman and political leader who served as the Fifty-eighth United States Secretary of State under President Jimmy Carter, Muskie also served as the governor

of and US Senator for Maine. Bucky once published an op-ed piece, originally sent as a telegram, in the *New York Times,* "A Telegram to Senator Ed Muskie" (March 27, 1971), about renewable energy.

Libby Newman   p. 14
Founding curator of the Esther Klein Gallery.

Isamu Noguchi   p. 20
A Japanese American artist and landscape architect, Noguchi was known for his sculpture and public works. He also designed stage sets for various Martha Graham productions, as well as several mass-produced lamps and furniture pieces.

Gerard K. O'Neill   p. 63
An American physicist and space activist who was on the faculty of Princeton University, O'Neill invented the particle storage ring, a device used in high-energy physics experiments.

Steve Parker   pp. 8, 53, 90
A producer, known for *My Geisha, John Goldfarb, Please Come Home!* and *The Dinah Shore Chevy Show,* Parker was married to Miki Hasegawa and Shirley MacLaine.

George and Eleanor Pavloff   pp. 48–51
Bed & breakfast pioneers, the Pavloffs founded the Goose Cove Lodge on Deer Isle, Maine, which was near Bucky's residence in Sunset.

Cedric Price   pp. 52, 102
An English architect and influential teacher and writer on architecture, Price was regarded as a visionary, with few built works to his credit. His realized projects include the 1961 London Zoo avlary, which he designed with Lord Snowdon and Frank Newby, and the Interaction Center in Kentish Town in London a decade later.

Kariska Pulchalski   p. 64
A teacher, creator of jewelry from sea glass, and herbalist, Pulchalski has been extensively involved for decades with the care and management of Bear Island. She is the daughter of Fuller's younger sister, Rosy.

Sam Rosenberg   p. 109
A writer and photographer best known for his 1974 study of Sherlock Holmes, titled *Naked Is the Best Disguise* (subtitled *The Death and Resurrection of Sherlock Holmes*), Rosenberg's other notable book is *The Confessions of a Trivialist* (originally published as *The Come As You Are Masquerade Party*).

Harrison Salisbury   p. 43
An American journalist and the first regular *New York Times* correspondent in Moscow after World War II, Salisbury was among the earliest journalists to oppose the Vietnam War from North Vietnam in 1966; he is the author of twenty-nine books.

Shirley Sharkey   pp. 19, 63, 91, 99, 105, 107, 112
Sharkey worked with Fuller for many years and became his executive administrator until his passing in 1983. She moved to Philadelphia when Fuller relocated his office there.... And special thanks to husband Bill for the "more-with-less" approach to bachelor cooking when Shirley is on the road.

Peter Simoneaux   pp. 54, 55, 101
Volunteer member of Fuller's staff.

Jaime Snyder   pp. 110, 111
An educator, writer, filmmaker, and singer-songwriter; Snyder is the Executor of the Estate of Buckminster Fuller and cofounder of the Buckminster Fuller Institute. He is Fuller's grandson, and studied and worked closely with him until his passing in 1983.

Hester Stearns   p. 25
Bucky's sister-in-law and Anne's youngest sister; identical twin of Hope Watts.

Connie Thelander   p. 98
Worked for Fuller during the early years in Philadelphia. She moved to Philadelphia from Illinois specifically to work in Fuller's office, but after many years moved back to Illinois.

Thomas Tse-Kwai Zung   pp. 56, 57
President of Buckminster Fuller, Sadao and Zung Architects, Tse-Kwai Zung was the principal designer and project architect to architect Edward Durell Stone when he worked on the New Orleans International Trade Mart; the master plan for the United States Naval Academy at Annapolis; the General Motors Headquarters building in New York; and the John F. Kennedy Center for the Performing Arts in Washington, D.C.

Amei Wallach   p. 91
An art critic and filmmaker who wrote "Hanging Out with Bucky, Thinking Big" for the *New York Times,* Wallach also wrote the introduction to Fuller's *Tetrascroll.*

Hope Watts   p. 26
Bucky's sister-in-law and Anne Fuller's youngest sister; identical twin of Hester Stearns.

Kathryn Whitlow   p. 42
Member of the board of trustees at Clarke College, serving on the Student Life and Development committees.

Whit Whitlow   p. 42
President of the East Dubuque Savings Bank, Whitlow served as president of the Dubuque Area Chamber of Commerce and as chairman of the board of trustees of Clarke College, from which he received an honorary doctorate of law degree in 1977.

Special thanks to Shirley Sharkey for providing background on the contributors; as well as to John Ferry and Josh Pang of the Estate of Buckminster Fuller for their assistance in the preparation of the bios. Great appreciation to Lars for his inspiration to make this project happen; and to Max and all the Lars Müller Publishers team, who always bring so much care and skill to the crafting of books. Thanks to Buckminster Fuller Institute for their reprint of the 'Christmas Egg Nog' recipe. Am also very grateful to my wife, Cheryl Snyder, and my sister, Alexandra May, for their keen editorial suggestions. And finally, on behalf of my family, deepest gratitude to the dear friends who contributed pieces–and especially to Bucky's staff for all their devoted support of both Bucky and Anne.

Jaime Snyder

An initiative by Lars Müller
Commentary: Jaime Snyder
Coordination: Max Wild
Copyediting and proofreading: Keonaona Peterson
Reproduction: Integral Lars Müller, Martina Mullis
Printing: DZA Druckerei zu Altenburg, Germany
Paper: FocusBook ivory 1.5, 80 gsm

Lars Müller Publishers is supported by the Swiss Federal Office of Culture with a structural contribution for the years 2016–2020.

Lars Müller Publishers
Zürich, Switzerland
www.lars-mueller-publishers.com

ISBN 978-3-03778-643-7

Distributed in North America by ARTBOOK | D.A.P.
www.artbook.com

Printed in Germany